1
+
color graphics vol.2
2

1 + 2

color graphics vol.2

P·I·E BOOKS
Villa Phoenix Suite 301, 4-14-6, Komagome,
Toshima-ku, Tokyo 170-0003 Japan
Tel: 03-3940-8302 Fax: 03-3576-7361
E-mail: piebooks@bekkoame.ne.jp

ISBN4-89444-093-8-C3070

First published in Germany 1999 by:
NIPPAN / Nippon Shuppan Hanbai Deutschland GmbH
Krefelder Straße 85, D-40549 Düsseldorf, Germany
Tel: 0211-5048080/89 Fax: 0211-5049326

ISBN 3-931884- 30-9

Printed in Japan

"1色＆2色デザイン"について、本書内に掲載されている3名のデザイナーに自由にコメントしていただきました。

As an introduction to this collection,we offer here the comments of three designers on the subject "design with one or two colors".

Als Vorwort zu dieser Sammlung präsentieren wir Ihnen die Kommentare von sechs Designern über das Thema „Design mit ein oder zwei Farben".

FOREWORD

Philip Fass

1～2色のデザインにおいては、非常に強い創造性が要求される。4色のように見た目の豪華さや、慣れ親しんだ使い勝手の良さに依存することができないからである。1～2色のデザインにおけるヒエラルキーと価値の構造は、ますます重要になっている。すなわち、プロジェクトの特定の課題に取り組みながら、選択された色の本来の特質をうまく利用し、真に強さのあるデザインにしなければならない、というものである。

次世代のデザインでは、技術の進化のスピードもあり、電子フォームがその重要性と利用範囲において、さらに隆盛を極めるであろう。しかし私は、印刷そのものが終焉を迎えるとは思わない。われわれの目は光を映し出す環境のもとで進化してきた。そして人々は、光を映すものを見たり、手に取ったりするのが好きなのである。コンピューターのスクリーンを見るのは、その方法のみに限定された単に1種類の視覚体験に過ぎない。また、1～2色デザインの美が、どのようにビデオ、映画や広告など他のビジュアル・フォームに影響を及ぼしたかを観察するのは興味深いものである。

1 & 2 color design demands strong creativity since it cannot rely on the flash or comfortable familiarity of 4 color process. The hierarchy and value structure in 1 & 2 color design becomes that much more important—it must be formally strong and take intelligent advantage of the intrinsic attributes of the colors chosen while addressing the specific issues of a project.
As for the next era of design, with the speed of technological development, electronic forms will continue to grow in importance and outreach. However, I don't believe print will die. Our eyes evolved in an environment that reflects light, and people like looking at and holding objects that reflect light. Looking into a computer screen is merely one kind of visual experience limited in its own way. Also, it's interesting to observe how 1 & 2 color aesthetics have influenced other visual forms such as video, film & advertising.

1 & 2 Farb-Design erfordert besondere Kreativität, da es sich nicht auf den Glanz und die bequeme Vertrautheit der Vierfarbsatz-Farben verlassen kann. Die Hierachie und Wertestruktur im 1 & 2 Farb-Design wird um so wichtiger – sie muss formell stark sein und bei der Lösung der speziellen Probleme des Projekts auf intelligente Weise Vorteil nehmen von den, den ausgewählten Farben innewohnenden Eigenschaften.
Durch die Schnelligkeit der technologischen Entwicklung werden in der nächsten Ära des Design elektronische Medien an Bedeutung und Reichweite gewinnen. Trotzdem glaube ich nicht, dass der Druck aussterben wird. Unsere Augen sind entstanden für eine Umwelt, die Licht reflektiert. Und Leute mögen es, Objekte zu halten und zu betrachten, die Licht reflektieren. Auf einen Computerbildschirm zu schauen, ist kaum eine dieser visuellen Erfahrungen - ist diese Erfahrung doch auf ihre eigene Weise limitiert. Es ist auch interessant zu beobachten, wie die 1 & 2 Farbästhetik andere visuelle Formen wie Video, Film und Werbung beeinflusst hat.

PROFILE

アメリカ合衆国の北アイオワ大学でグラフィック・デザインを教えている。その作品は、国内および国際的に発表されている。また、個人的にも多くの作品をつくり、作品集も制作している。アルバナ・シャンペーンのイリノイ大学より、MFAを取得。大学では、佐藤しょうぞう氏から日本の美学、郡司きみこ氏から生け花（池の坊）を学んだ。

Philip Fass teaches graphic design in the United States at The University of Northern Iowa. He design work has been published internationally and nationally. He also does personal creative work and artist's books.
He received his MFA from The University of Illinois at Urbana-Champaign. While there he studied Japanese Aesthetics with Shozo Sato, and Ikebana (Ikenobo style) with Kimiko Gunji.

Philip Fass lehrt Graphik-Design in den USA an der Universität von Nord Iowa. Seine Design-Arbeiten wurden national wie international veröffentlicht. Er berät auch in Kreativ-Angelegenheit und macht Bücher über Künstler.
Er hat einen Abschluss der Universität von Illinois in Urbana-Champaign. Dort studierte er japanische Ästhetik bei Shozo Sato und Ikebana im Ikenobo-Stil bei Kimiko Gunji.

Melchior Imboden

本書のコンセプトである「1〜2色のデザイン」は、まさに新たな世紀を迎えようとする現在、特に重要なコンセプトである。コンピューターの導入はグラフィック・デザインを大きく変化させ、無制限といってよいほどの新しい機会をもたらした。この巨大なアリーナでどのように動くべきかを選択することは、私たちにとって新しい課題である。だからこそ、少ない色数で製作された、厳選されたデザインを紹介することは意義が深い。予算の削減により、色数を制限して印刷物をつくらなければならない場合が多い。デザイナーにとって、洗練されたイメージを選択しながら少ない色数によって、意識的に限定されたアプリケーションとその理解の世界を築き上げるのは非常に難しい。シンプルさは現実と組み合わさって、しばしば特別なパワーを発揮する。今日の限定色の作品が、21世紀になってもその魅力を失うことがなければ、私たちはデザイナーとして目標を達成したと言える。

The concept of this book project, "1 & 2 Color Design," is a particularly important one, especially in a time with the next millennium on the horizon. Since the introduction of the computer, graphic design has changed rapidly, and an almost unlimited number of new opportunities have opened up. The choices of how to move within this vast arena pose new challenges to us. That is why the idea to present selected designs, created with a reduced number of colors, is a great one. Reduced cost is often a reason for producing printed matter with limited colors. I believe that it is a particularly difficult challenge for a designer to create his own field of willingly reduced application and comprehension by the limitation of color in combination with a selection of sophisticated images. Simplicity combined with actuality is often a source of special power. If we can carry today's limited color printed pieces into the next millennium without having them lose their attraction, then we as Designers will have reached our target.

Die Idee des Buchprojektes 1 & 2 Color Design, finde ich von besonderer Wichtigkeit, insbesondere in einer Zeit in welcher wir uns in ein neues Jahrtausend begeben. Seit der Einführung des Computers hat sich auch das Grafik-Design entschieden verändert und gleichzeitig haben sich scheinbar unbegrenzte neue Möglichkeiten geöffnet. Die Wahl, sich in diesem weiten Feld zu bewegen, stellt uns vor neue Herausforderungen. Gerade deshalb ist der Gedanke, ausgewählte Arbeiten mittels reduzierter Farbauswahl entstandener Werke in diesem Buch zu vereinen, eine grossartige Idee. Der Grund, eine Drucksache mit reduzierter Anzahl von Farben anzufertigen, liegt oft in den tieferen Druckkosten. Ich denke, gerade dies kann für eine Gestalterin oder einen Gestalter ein besonders grosser Anreiz sein, sich mittels eingeschränkter Farbwahl in Verbindung mit gezielt raffinierter Formkombination ein eigenes Feld von bewusst reduzierter Anwendug und Auffassung zu schaffen. Oft liegt in der Einfachheit vereint mit der Aktualität eine ganz besondere Stärke. Wenn wir unsere jetzt erstellten, mittels reduzierten Farben entstandenen Druckerzeugnisse ins nächste Jahrtausend rüberretten können und sie auch in nächster Zukunft nichts an Aktualität verlieren werden, haben wir unser als Designer angestrebtes Ziel erreicht.

PROFILE

1956年スイスのスタンスに生まれる。ルツェルンアートスクールにてグラフィックデザインを学んだ後、92年自らのスタジオを設立。94年第16回ブルノ国際グラフィックビエンナーレ金賞、95年第11回ヘルシンキ国際ポスタービエンナーレ特別賞、96年第15回ワルシャワ国際ポスタービエンナーレ銀メダル、96年モスクワGolden Bee 3における世界ポスター受賞者コンペティションIBCC賞第1位など受賞歴多数。

Born in Stans, Switzerlan in 1956. He studied graphic design at the art school of Lucerne and started his own graphic studio in 1992.
His art exhibition posters have been awarded several prizes; for example, 1994 Gold medal at the 16th international poster biennial in Brno, 1995 Honourable mention at the 11th international poster biennial in Helsinki, 1996 Silver medal at the 15th international poster biennial in Helsinki, 1996 first prize IBCC award the the worlds poster winners competition at the Golden Bee 3 in Moscow.

Heather Heflin

現在までのところ、私は（クライアントが知りうる限りでは）、予算の限定のため、1〜2色の作品を最も多く造ってきた。しかし、ここ数年デジタル印刷があまりにも（経済的に）身近になり、多くのクライアントはこの方法を選択するようになってきている。なぜなら、通常のオフセット印刷と同じ程度の金額で、「より以上」のもの（つまり色）を手にすることができると思っているためである。クライアントの多くは、フルカラーであることが作品の最高のクオリティと美に等しいものであると考えているかのようである。私は、選択肢として無限の、色のスペクトルに何らかの有利な点はいまだ見い出せていないし、こういった４色の作品よりもむしろ、1〜2色の作品を造りたいとさえ思っている。1〜2色のデザインをデザイン・プロセスの限定とは見ていない。むしろ、それぞれの色の特色を学び、たとえばフォルムといった他の重要な面に集中できる良い機会と捉えている。印刷物のなかでふんだんに使われた色が、作品の重要な要素を破壊しているに過ぎない例を幾度となく見てきた。最低の色数でデザインすることが制約と受け取られるなら、あえて私はこちらを選びたい。制約は時には有効なものである。なぜならそれは、私たちにシステムや日常を逸脱するよう促し、隠れたリソースを発見、あるいは「裸に」させるからである。

Up until now, (as far as clients know) it has most often been because of a limited budget that I have produced work that is 1-2 colors. But 4-color digital printing has become so accessible (financially) in the last couple of years that many clients are opting for this method because they feel they are getting "more" (color) for almost the same amount of money as regular offset. It seems as if many clients feel that full-color equates to quality and beauty in a piece. As for me, I do not yet see the advantage of having an unlimited spectrum from which to choose-I would much rather produce one to two color work over these 4-color pieces. I do not perceive 1-2-color work as the result of a limitation on the design process, but rather an opportunity to really study individual colors and to also concentrate on other important aspects, such as form. So many times I think that the abundance of colors that I see in printed work do nothing more than distract from the formal elements of a piece! If designing with a minimum number of colors is viewed as a constraint, then I still opt for this. Constraint is useful in that it forces us out of a system or routine, and compels us to discover, or UNCOVER, hidden resources.

Bis heute (soweit meine Kunden wissen) waren es meist Budgetbeschränkungen, weswegen ich Arbeiten in ein und zwei Farben produzierte. Aber der Vierfarb-Digitaldruck wurde in den letzten Jahren (finanziell) so erschwinglich, dass viele Kunden für dieses Verfahren optieren, weil sie glauben, „mehr"(Farbe) für fast das gleiche Geld wie beim regulären Offset zu bekommen. Es scheint, als meinten die Kunden, volle Farbe stehe für Qualität und Schönheit einer Drucksache. Ich für mich sehe die Vorteile der Auswahl aus einem unlimitierten Farbspektrum nicht. Ich würde lieber ein- und zweifarbige Arbeiten produzieren als vierfarbige. Ich empfinde 1-2-Farb-Arbeiten als Limitation im Design-Prozess. Ich sehe es eher als Gelegenheit, die individuellen Farben wirklich zu studieren und mich auch auf andere wichtige Aspekte wie die Form zu konzentrieren. Wie oft denke ich, da der Überfluss an Farben, die ich in Druckwerken sehe, nichts anderes tut, als von den formalen Elementen eines Stückes abzulenken! Wenn das Gestalten mit einer minimalen Farbanzahl als Beschränkung angesehen wird, so bin ich trotzdem dafür. Beschränkung ist nützlich, denn sie zwingt uns aus einem System oder aus der Routine, und verdammt uns, zu entdecken, verborgene Ressourcen zu finden und zu nutzen.

PROFILE

ワシントン州シアトルの NBBJ グラフィック・デザイン勤務。コーニッシュ・カレッジ・オブ・アーツのグラフィック・デザイン部門で教えている。

I now work for NBBJ Graphic Design in Seattle, Washington and also teach in the Graphic Design Department at Cornish College of the Arts.

Ich arbeite jetzt für NBBJ in Seattle, Washington, und lehre auch an der Graphik-Design-Abteilung des Cornish College of the Arts.

EDITORIAL NOTES

CREDIT FORMAT

Creative Staff
 CD: Creative Director
 AD: Art Director
 D: Designer
 P: Photographer
 I: Illustrator
 CW: Copywriter
 PD: Producer
 DF: Design Firm
 C: Client

Country from which submitted /
Year of completion

With information provided by contributors, we have included the PANTONE® Color reference numbers, and corresponding color chips, of the printing inks used for each piece of artwork, as reference data next to each credit. For those few pieces for which this information was incomplete, we have identified the inks ourselves. As this book has been printed in four colors, the colors may vary slightly from that of the actual printing inks.

Special printing processes are identified by the following symbols:

*H: Hot Stamp
*T: Thermography
*E: Embossing

PANTONE® Color references are protected by copyright and are reproduced herein by permission of Pantone, Inc. PANTONE-identified Color reproduction information has been provided for the guidance of the reader. The colors have not been checked by Pantone, Inc. for accuracy. Refer to current PANTONE Color Publications for the color standard. PANTONE® is a registered trademark of Pantone, Inc.

出品者から送付された情報をもとに、作品に使用された印刷インクの参考資料として、各クレジットの横にパントーンナンバーと色チップを掲載しました。
出品者からの情報が不足している一部の作品については、小社で判断しました。
本書は4色のプロセスカラーで印刷されていますので、実際の印刷インクとは多少異なる参考程度の資料であることをあらかじめご了承ください。
また、再現が難しい特殊加工については、下記記号で表記しました。

＊H: Hot Stamp / 箔押し
＊T: Thermography / バーコ印刷
＊E: Embossing / 型押し

PANTONE®のカラーリファレンスは著作権により保護されており、本書においてはPANTONE社の許諾を得て複製しています。
PANTONEによるカラーの複製情報が、読者の参考までに掲載されています。
これらのカラーは、PANTONE社によって正確さをチェックされたものではありません。カラー標準に関しては、現在発行中のPANTONEカラー・パブリケーションをご参照ください。
PANTONE®は、PANTONE社の登録商標です。

CONTENTS

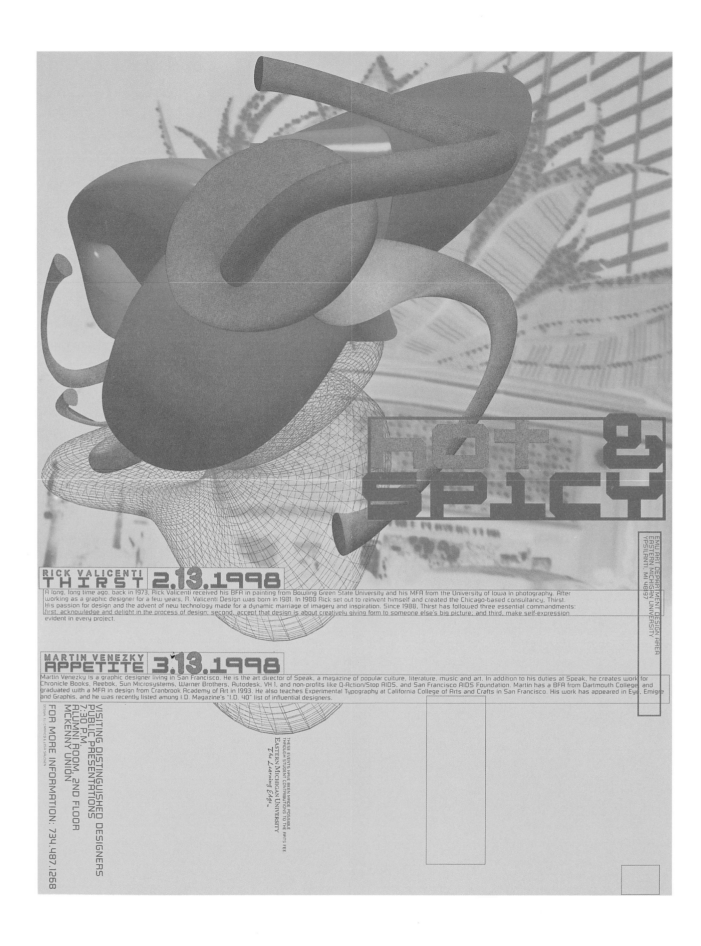

PANTONE Process Magenta C
PANTONE 8202 C

CD, AD, D: Liisa Salonen D, P, I: Eli Carrico DF: Design Department, Eastern Michigan University CL: Eastern Michigan University
Canada 1998

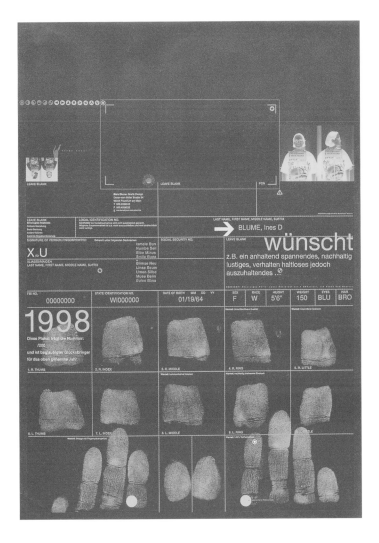

D: Ines Blume (1. 2) Dagmar Schneider (2) DF, CL: Ines Blume. Delikate Gestaltung   Germany 1997

PANTONE Process Magenta C
PANTONE Process Yellow C
PANTONE 804 C

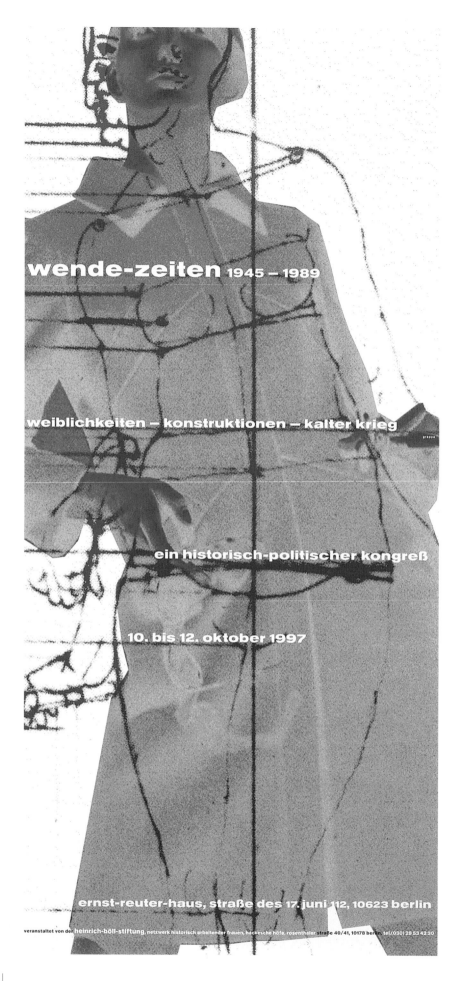

PANTONE 1235 U
PANTONE 2767 U

D: Heike Grebin DF: Grappa Blotto CL: Heinrich - Böu - Sttetung   Germany 1997

D: Dieter Peseke DF: Grappa Blotto + Dor CL: Bauhaus Dessau   Germany 1996

PANTONE 111 C
PANTONE 2728 C

Jahrestreffen 1997 – René Dalpra · Peter Felder · Hans-Joachim Gögl

Das Ideal liegt in dir. Das Hindernis auch. *Thomas Carlyle*

Physiotherapie **Bert Nab**

PANTONE Yellow 012 U | CD, AD, D, DF: René Dalpra P: Hugo Ender CW: Haktmut Hofer CL: Community of Götzis   Austria 1998

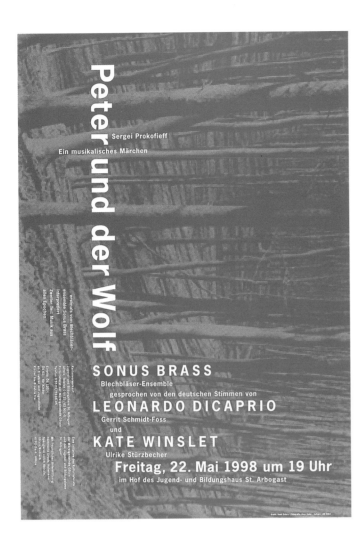

1. CD, AD, D, P, DF: René Dalpra D: Dominik Zumtobel CL: Bert Nab   Austria 1997

PANTONE 355 U

2. D: Peter Felder P: Stadtarchiv der Stadt Dornbirn CW: Marina Hämmerle DF: Felder Grafikdesign
CL: Zentralvereinigung der Architekten Österreichs   Austria 1996

PANTONE Process Black U
PANTONE 354 U

D, P, CW, DF: Cyan CL: Bauhaus Dessau Foundation   Germany 1997 - 98

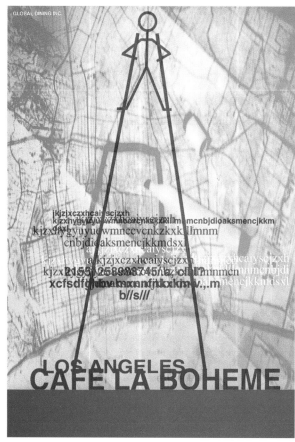

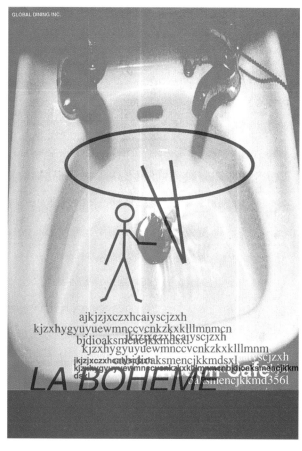

PANTONE 192 C
PANTONE Process Cyan C

AD, D, I: Tatsuo Ebina P: Tadashi Tomono DF: E Co. , Ltd. CL: Global Dining Inc.   Japan 1996

spiritual

Nigel Curtiss

material

Nigel Curtiss

CD, CW: Bob Ward   AD: Osamu Fukushima   D: Naoki Bando   I: Masaaki Okino   CL: Nigel Curtiss   Japan 1997

PANTONE 425 C
PANTONE Process Black C

This conference made possible by the support of the Cultural Services of the French Embassy

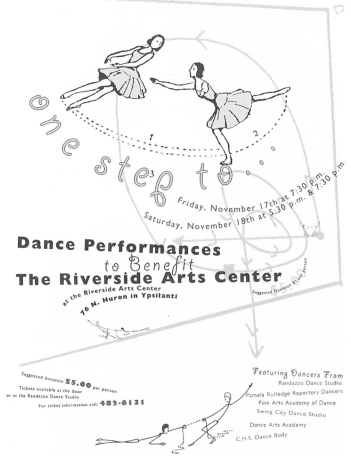

PANTONE 301 U
PANTONE Red 032 U

1. CD, D: Bjorn Akselsen DF: Icehouse Design CL: Yale University / French Department   USA 1997

PANTONE 1817 U
PANTONE 196 U

2. D: Gail Salenbien / Michelle Gould DF: Student Project CL: The Riverside Arts Center   USA 1995

1. CD, AD: Roxy Moffit D, I: Michael Strassburger DF: Modern Dog CL: Seattle Repertory Theatre   USA 1997

PANTONE 4655 U

PANTONE Process Black U

2. CD, AD, D, I: Robynne Raye DF: Modern Dog CL: Seattle Center   USA 1997

PANTONE 4525 C

PANTONE Process Black C

1

2

kirimax!

PANTONE Reflex Blue C
PANTONE Red 032 C

1. AD, D:Harumi Kirima DF, CL: Kirima Design Office   Japan 1998

PANTONE 877 C
PANTONE Process Black C

2. AD, D: Harumi Kirima D: Fumitaka Yukawa DF: Kirima Design Office CL: Pia Corporation   Japan 1996

PANTONE Black 6 C 2X
PANTONE 1375 C

PANTONE Black 6 C 2X
PANTONE 194 C

PANTONE Black 6 C 2X
PANTONE 135 C

CD: Juan Cravero AD: Sebastian Olivieri D: Marcela Augustowsky I: Niño Rodríguez CW: Fernando Negro Arrosi DF: Young & Rubicam Argentina CL: Metropolitan Life   Argentina 1998

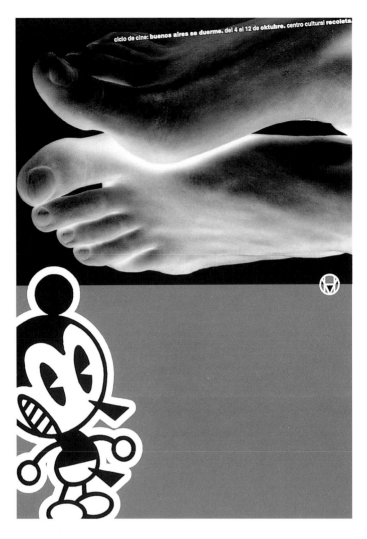

 PANTONE Black 6 C 2X
PANTONE 1655 C

PANTONE Black 6 C 2X
PANTONE 1215 C

CD, AD, D: Marcela Augustowsky P: Jorge Truscello I: Niño Rodríguez DF: Augustowsky Design
CL: Centro Cultural Recoleta   Argentina 1997

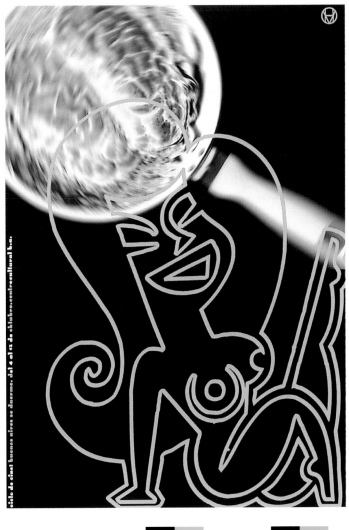

CD, AD, D: Marcela Augustowsky   P: Jorge Truscello   I: Niño Rodríguez   DF: Augustowsky Design   CL: Centro Cultural Recoleta   Argentina   1997

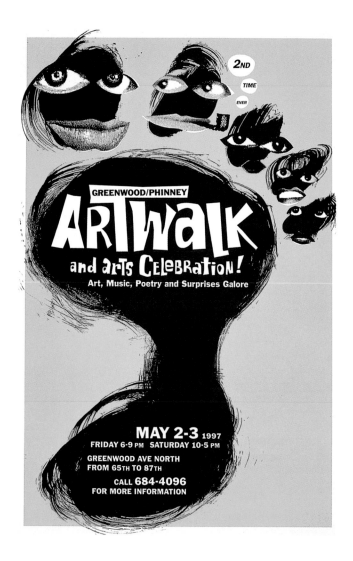

PANTONE 115 U
PANTONE Process Black U

1. CD, AD, D, I: Robynne Raye DF: Modern Dog CL: Greenwood Arts Council   USA 1997

PANTONE 110 C
PANTONE 187 U

2. CD, AD: Roxy Moffit D, I: Vittorio Costarella DF: Modern Dog CL: The Long Wharf Theatre   USA 1997

3. CD, AD, D, I: Vittorio Costarella DF: Modern Dog CL: Greenwood Arts Council   USA 1998

PANTONE 166 C
PANTONE 549 C

4. CD, AD, D, I: Vittorio Costarella DF: Modern Dog CL: Moe Cafe   USA 1995

PANTONE 1665 C
PANTONE 356 C

PANTONE Black 6 C 2X
PANTONE 1345 C

CD, AD, D: Marcela Augustowsky AD, I: Max Cachimba DF: Augustowsky Design CL: Max Cachimba   Argentina 1997

1. AD, D, I: Jun Furukawa CW: Hiroko Kurita CL: McCann - Erickson Inc.   Japan 1997

PANTONE 310 U
PANTONE 5425 U

2. AD: Joshua Berger / Niko Courtelis / Pete McCracken D: Petra Wenneberg DF: Plazm CL: Plazm Magazine   USA 1995

PANTONE Process Black C
PANTONE Red 032 C

PANTONE Process Black U
PANTONE 485 U

1. D: Paul Gillis I: Martina Witte DF: NBBJ Graphic Design CL: Empty Space Theatre   USA 1998

PANTONE Process Black C

2. CD, AD, D, I, CW: Pedro Yamashita   Japan 1996

PANTONE Process Black C
PANTONE 877 C

3. D, I, CW: Afei Kitahana CL: Blue Heaven Pools   Japan 1998

1. CD, D, P: Hiroyuki Nagashima AD: Toru Onozato DF: Design Factory Millennium CL: Avant Guerre   Japan 1996

PANTONE 1787 C
PANTONE 3395 C

CD, AD, D, DF: Joerg Waschat CL: Pace Agency   Germany 1996

PANTONE 4625 U

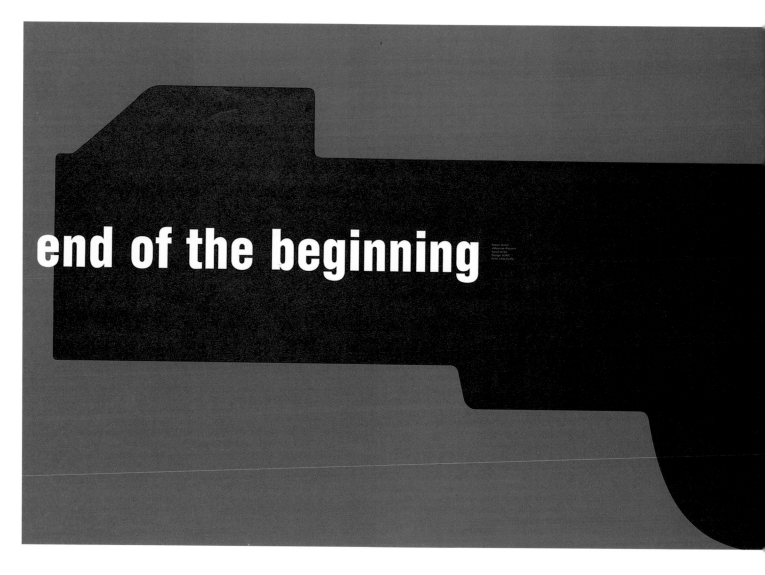

end of the beginning

wear condoms. don't give aids a single chance.
esperanza de vida fundation.

PANTONE 200 C
PANTONE Process Black C

1. CD, AD, D, I: Yuri Surkov DF, CL: Suric Design   Russia 1995

PANTONE 174 C
PANTONE Warm Red C

2. CD, CW: Juan Cravero AD, CW: Dario Lanis AD, D: Marcela Augustowsky I: Max Cachimba DF: Young & Rubicam
CL: Esperanza de Vidafundation   Argentina 1996

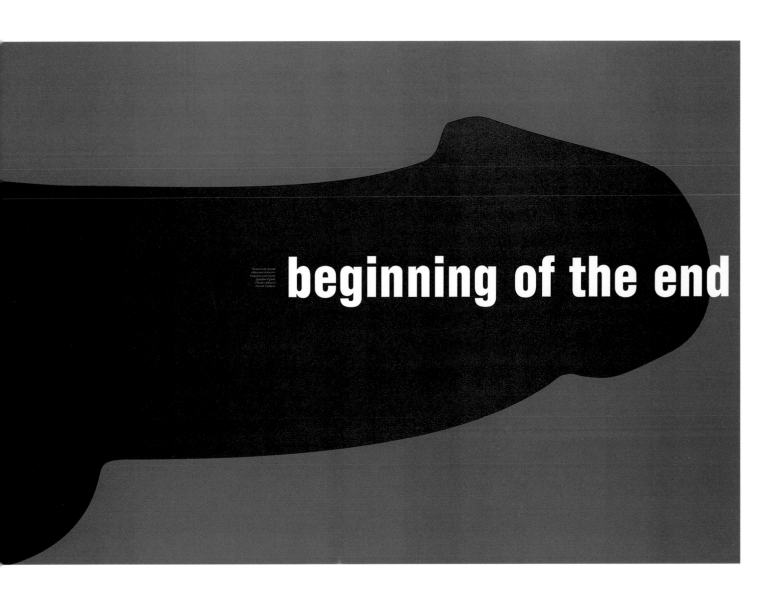

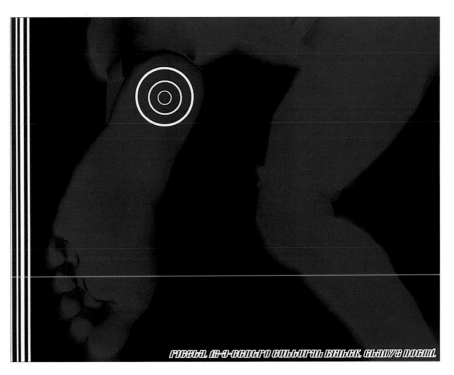

3. CD, AD, D, I: Marcela Augustowsky I: 3D Image DF: Augustowsky Design CL: Gladys Noemi   Argentina 1997

PANTONE Black 6 C 2X
PANTONE Reflex Blue C

 PANTONE 1797 C
PANTONE 2768 C

 PANTONE 179 U
PANTONE 280 U

AD, D: Tirso Francés / Dylan Fracareta AD: Ron Faas P: Divers DF: Dietwee CL: Mojo Concerts   Netherlands 1998

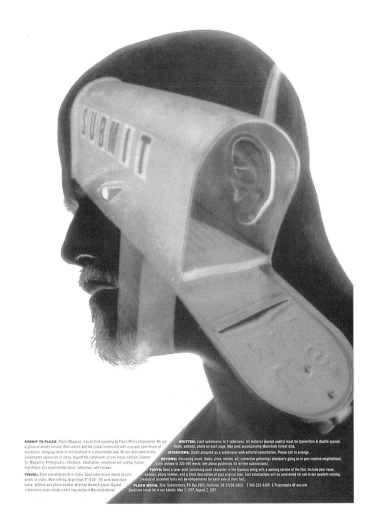

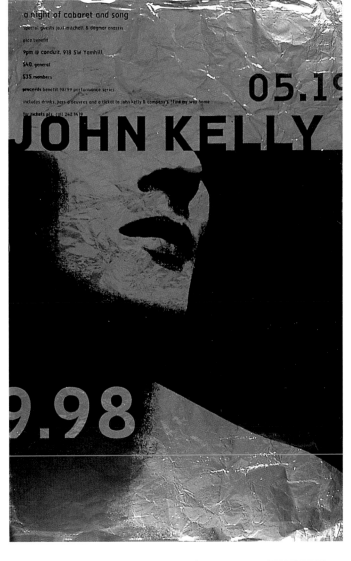

1. AD, D: Niko Courtelis P: Bob Waldman Head: Robert Rasmussen DF: Plazm CL: Plazm Magazine   USA 1997

2. AD, D: Enrique Mosqueda D: Kirsty Munn CL: Portland Institute for Contemporary Art   USA 1998

> images design joe be ker, pascal béjean // 1997

RANDOM ACCESS

[6 EGREES OF PERCEPTION]

 PANTONE Process Black U
White

CD, AD, D, P, CW: Jue Becker / Pascal Béjean CL: Bulldozer®éditions   France 1997

1. D: Andreas Trogisch / D. Peseke DF: Grappa Blotto + Dor CL: Maxim Gorki Theater   Germany 1997

PANTONE 1788 U
PANTONE 2767 U

2. D: Grebin / Warner DF: Grappa Blotto CL: Eco Direkt - Umwelt Aktionen for Berlin   Germany 1997

PANTONE 1788 U
PANTONE 2767 U

From the Spoon to the City: An Evening with Lella and Massimo Vignelli

AigANY

Wednesday October 16 1996 7pm The Katie Murphy Amphitheatre at FIT

AIGA/NY Members $10 Public $15 All Students with ID $5 FIT Students $0

BAUHAUS DESSAU 25.1. - 22.3.1998
ERÖFFNUNG AM 24.1.1998 UM 17 UHR

1899-1986

ARCHITEKT-VISIONÄR-GESTALTER

MART STAM

Stiftung Bauhaus Dessau Sammlung Gropiusallee 38 D-00846 Dessau Telefon 0340-6508-210 Fax 0340-6508-218

PANTONE Process Black U
PANTONE 484 U

1, D: J. Graham Hanson / Massimo Vignelli DF: Vignelli Associates CL: American Institute of Graphic Arts, New York USA 1996

PANTONE Orange 021 U
PANTONE 371 U

2, D, P, CW, DF: Cyan CL: Bauhaus Dessau Foundation Germany 1998

1. CD, AD, D: Imboden Melchior DF: Imboden Melchior Grafik Atelier CL: City of Stans   Switzerland 1997

PANTONE Red 032 C
PANTONE Process Black C

2. CD, AD, D: Yuri Surkov DF: Suric Design CL: Berliner Ensemble and Designer association VGD   Russia 1997

PANTONE 179 C
PANTONE Process Black C

PANTONE Process Black C
PANTONE Red 032 C

AD, D, DF: Kijuro Yahagi CL: The Organizing Commitee of International Symposium "Le Corbusier & Japan" Japan 1997

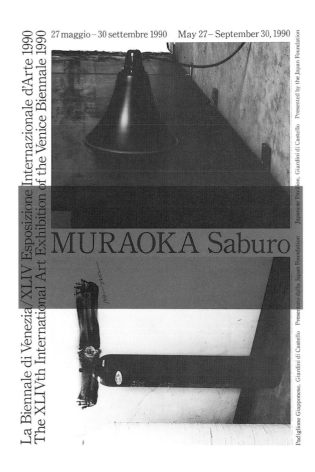

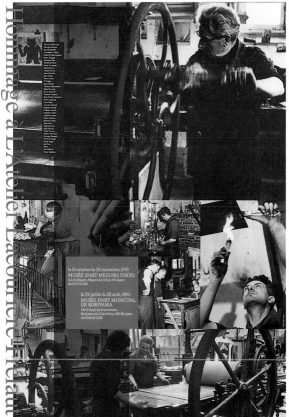

1. 2. AD, D, DF: Kijuro Yahagi CL: The Japan Foundation   Japan 1990

PANTONE Process Black C
PANTONE 1788 C

3. AD, D, DF: Kijuro Yahagi CL: Meguro Museum of Art   Japan 1993

PANTONE Process Black C
PANTONE 1788 C

PANTONE Process Black U
PANTONE Red 185 U

1. CD, AD, D, P: Liisa Salonen I: El Lissitzky DF: Design Department, Cranbrook Academy of Art CL: Cranbrook Art Museum   Canada 1995

PANTONE Process Black C
PANTONE Warm Red C

2. CD, D: Charles Shields AD: Stephanie Wong P: Joel Pickford DF: Shields Design CL: Art for Aids   USA 1997

1. CD, AD, D, P: Imboden Melchior DF: Imboden Melchior Grafik Atelier CL: IHA Hergiswil   Switzerland 1998

PANTONE Red 032 C
PANTONE Process Black C

2. AD: Joshua Berger / Niko Courtelis / Pete McCracken D: Alex Trub DF: Plazm CL: Plazm Magazine   USA 1996

PANTONE 1797 C
PANTONE Process Black C

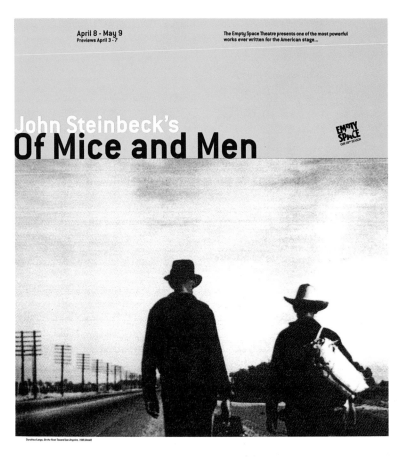

PANTONE Process Black U
PANTONE 382 U

1. D: Heike Grebin DF: Grappa Blotto CL: Filmverband Brandenburg e.v.   Germany 1996

PANTONE Process Black U
PANTONE 396 U

2. D: Leo Raymundo P: Dorothea Lange DF: NBBJ Graphic Design CL: Empty Space Theatre   USA 1998

1. CD, AD, D, DF: Joerg Waschat CL: Pace Agency   Germany 1996

2. CD: Steven Sikora D: Richard Boynton P: Darrell Eager DF: Design Guys CL: Public Radio International   USA 1996

PANTONE Process Black C
PANTONE Red 032 C

CD, P: Georg Alfare CD, AD, D: Peter Felder CW: Klaus Tschanett DF: Felder Grafikdesign CL: Gemeinde Schlins / Jugendreferat   Austria 1997

CD, AD, D: Ryan McGinness CW: Saturnine DF: Ryan McGinness Studio CL: Saturnine / Victorialand Records   USA 1998

PANTONE 809 U
PANTONE Process Cyan U
PANTONE 2766 U

PANTONE 342 U
PANTONE 874 U

1. AD, D: Péter Vajda CL: Szabad Tér Színház   Hungary 1996

PANTONE Process Black C
PANTONE 871 C

2. D, P, CW, DF: Cyan CL: State Opera Berlin   Germany 1998

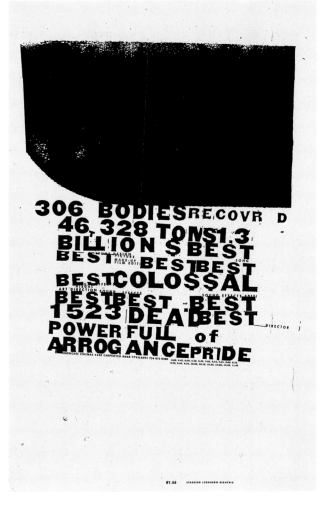

1. CD, AD, D, DF: André M. Baldinger CL: Federal Office of Culture   Switzerland 1997

2. D, I: Andy Beach   USA 1998

still life

naturemorte

stilleben

чернобыль

PANTONE Process Black C
PANTONE 101 C

CD, AD, D, I: Yuri Surkov DF: Suric Design CL: Suric Design   Russia 1996

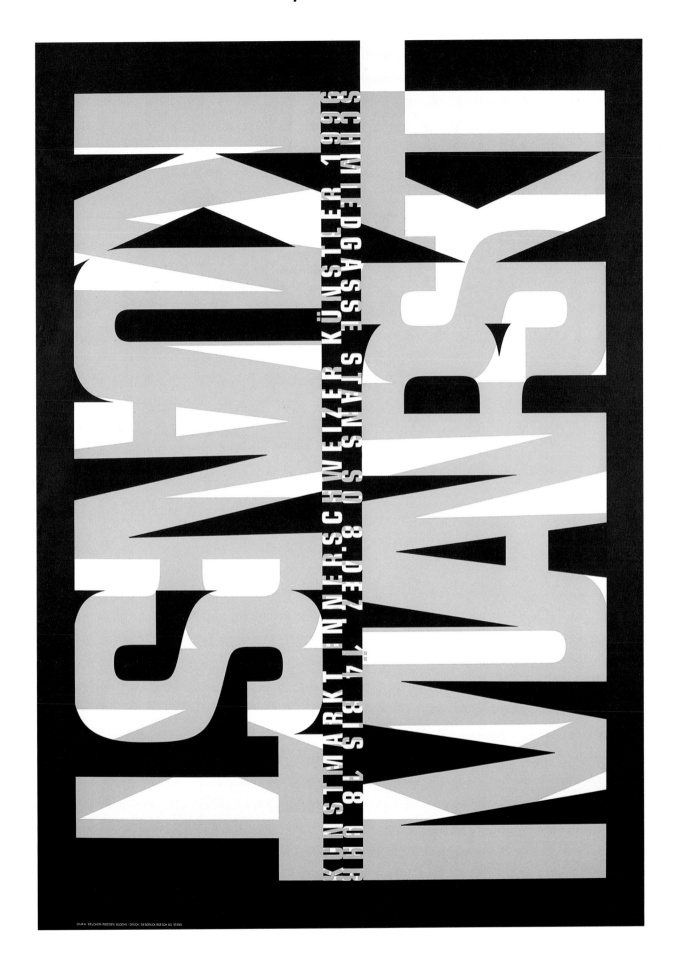

CD, AD, D: Imboden Melchior DF: Imboden Melchior Grafik Atelier CL: City of Stans Switzerland 1996

PANTONE 382 C
PANTONE Process Black C

1

2

Siedepunkt erreicht? - Kein Grund zu schlagen

Siedepunkt erreicht? - Kein Grund zu schlagen

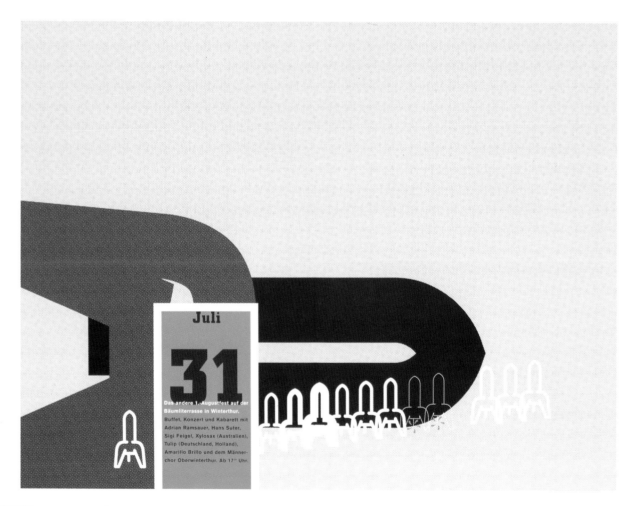

PANTONE Process Black C
PANTONE 397 C

1. CD, AD, D: Kerstin Antony DF: Büro für gestaltung   Germany 1997

PANTONE Process Black U
PANTONE Orange 021 U

2. D: Thomas Bruggisser DF: Grafiktraktor CL: Urs Akeret   Switzerland 1997

Michelangelo Buonarroti

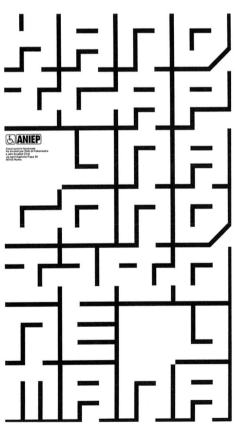

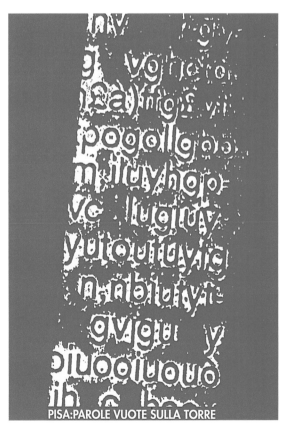

PISA:PAROLE VUOTE SULLA TORRE

1. CD, AD, D : Gianni Bortolotti DF: Studio Gianni Bortolotti & C. s. a. s. CL: Comune di Bologna   Italy 1998   PANTONE Process Black U

2. CD, AD, D : Gianni Bortolotti DF: Studio Gianni Bortolotti & C. s. a. s. CL: ANIEP   Italy 1995   PANTONE Process Black U

3. CD, AD, D : Gianni Bortolotti DF: Studio Gianni Bortolotti & C. s. a. s. CL: Comitato di Difesa Della Torre   Italy 1997   PANTONE Process Blue U

PANTONE 2745 U
PANTONE 396 U | D: Jennifer Moody / Gail Swanlund   P: Mat Roe   DF: Nice Design   CL: California Institute of the Arts, Office of Admissions   USA 1996

1. D, I: Peter Felder CW: Johannes Rauch DF: Felder Grafikdesign CL: Plattform Für ein M. A. I. - Freies Österreich Austria 1998

PANTONE Process Black C
White

2. CD: Lionello Borean Account: Stefano Dal Tin D: Owen M. Walters DF: Metalli Lindberg Adv. CL: Quartiere Latino Italy 1998

PANTONE Process Black C
PANTONE 384 C

PANTONE Process Black C

1. CD, AD, D: Imboden Melchior P: Leonard Von Matt DF: Imboden Melchior Grafik Atelier CL: City of Lucerne   Switzerland 1995

PANTONE Process Black C
PANTONE 450 C

2. CD, AD, D: Imboden Melchior P: Martin Imboden DF: Imboden Melchior Grafik Atelier CL: City of Stans   Switzerland 1997

1. CD, AD, D: Charles Shields P: Keith Seaman - Camerad DF: Shields Design CL: Art for Aids   USA 1996

2. CD: Charles Shields AD: Stephanie Wong D: Rachel Browns I: Robert Ogata DF: Shields Design CL: Art for Aids   USA 1998

PANTONE 506 U
PANTONE 456 U

PANTONE 1245 U
PANTONE 2592 U

D: Kees Wagenaars   DF: Case   CL: Coc / Chassé Cinema   Netherlands 1997(1) 1998(2)

PANTONE 1925 C
PANTONE 2745 C
PANTONE 382 C
PANTONE 548 C

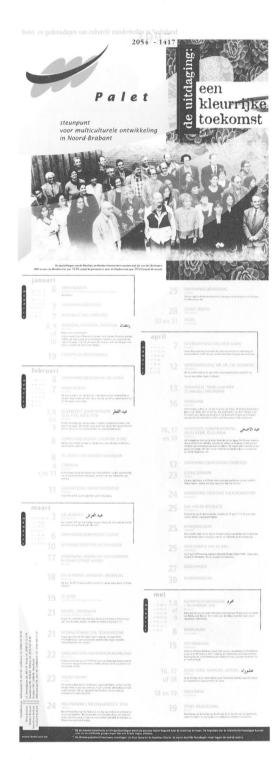

1. CD: Lionello Borean Account: Stefano Dal Tin DF: Metalli Lindberg Adv. CL: Associazione Prosa / PN   Italy 1998

PANTONE Process Black U

PANTONE 174 U

2. CD, AD, D, I: Martha Lauría P: Frank Hardesmeets CW: Palet Foundation DF: Lauría Grafisch Ontwerp CL: Palet Foundation   Netherlands 1997

PANTONE 200 C

PANTONE 137 C

PANTONE 2765 U
PANTONE Orange 021 U

1. CD, AD, D: Wout de Vringer DF: Faydherbe / De Vringer CL: Intertext Bedrijfs Vertalingen   Netherlands 1997

PANTONE Process Black U
White

2. CD, AD, D, CW: Ralph Schraivogel DF: Schraivogel Design CL: Zurich Film Podium   Switzerland 1996

PANTONE 8543 C

3. D, P, CW: Pascal Béjean DF: La Bomatic CL: Béjean / Justôme   France 1998

1. CD, AD, D, CW: Ralph Schraivogel DF: Schraivogel Design CL: Zurich Film Podium   Switzerland 1998

PANTONE Process Black U
PANTONE 877 U

2. CD, AD, D, CW: Ralph Schraivogel P: Hugo Jaeggi DF: Schraivogel Design CL: Zurich Film Podium   Switzerland 1995

PANTONE Process Black U
White

3. CD, AD, D, CW: Ralph Schraivogel P: Peter Hunkeler DF: Schraivogel Design CL: Zurich Museum of Design   Switzerland 1997

PANTONE Process Black U
PANTONE 451 U

THE ROYAL FLUSH JAZZ BAND

 PANTONE Process Black C | AD, D: Ken Miki P: Kuninobu Fukuda DF: Ken Miki & Associates CL: The Royal Flush Jazz Band   Japan 1997

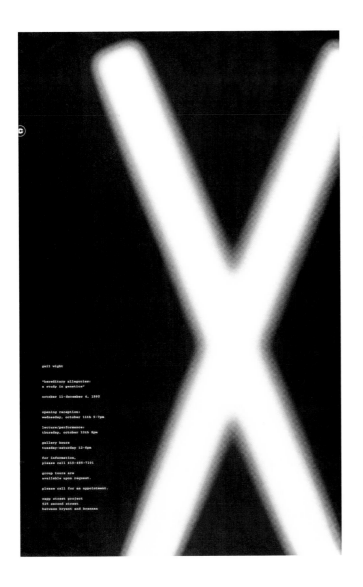

AD, D: Jennifer Morla D: Craig Bailey CW: Capp Street Project DF: Morla Design CL: Capp Street Project   USA 1995   PANTONE Process Black C

PANTONE Process Black C   AD, D: Jennifer Morla D: Craig Bailey CW: Capp Street Project DF: Morla Design CL: Capp Street Project   USA 1995

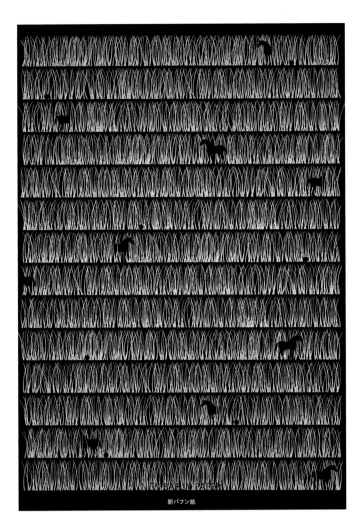

1. AD: Ken Miki D: Junji Osaki / Shigeyuki Sakaida P: Kuninobu Fukuda DF: Ken Miki & Associates CL: Heiwa Paper   Japan 1997   PANTONE Process Black U

2. AD, D: Jennifer Morla D: Craig Bailey CW: Capp Street Project DF: Morla Design CL: Capp Street Project   USA 1995   PANTONE Process Black C

IT'S "SNOOPY"

IT'S "SNOOPY"

PANTONE Process Black C.

AD, D: Yasumi Numajiri D: Megumi Kaneko / Chikako Hori P: Keita Miyanaga Stylist: Masato Okamura PD: Kazue Ito DF: Saito, Numajiri Design Office
CL: United Media K. K. Event: Happy Birthday SNOOPY in Parco   Japan 1996   PEANUTS © United Feature Syndicate, Inc.

PANTONE Process Black U
PANTONE 534 U

D, P, CW, DF: Cyan CL: Toula limnaios   Germany 1998

1, CD, AD, D: Philip Fass CW: Bettina Fabos CL: Cedar Arts Forum   USA 1997

PANTONE 188 C
PANTONE Process Black C

2, CD, AD, D: Philip Fass CL: University of Northern Iowa Department of Art   USA 1996

PANTONE 8602 C

PANTONE 478 U | CD, AD, D, I: Carlos Segura AD, D, I: Susana Detembleque I: Colin Metcalf DF: Segura Inc. CL: [T - 26] Digital Typefoundry   USA 1998

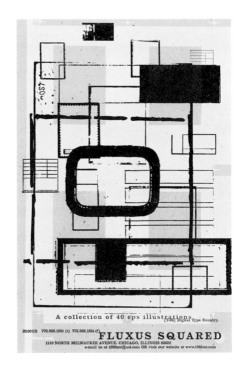

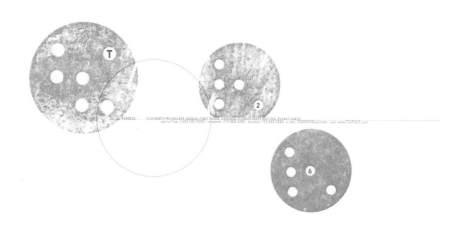

CD, AD, D: Carlos Segura D: John Rousseau DF: Segura Inc. CL: [T - 26] Digital Typefoundry USA 1997

PANTONE 165 U
PANTONE Process Black U

PANTONE 1665 C
PANTONE Process Black C

D: Trogisch / Grebin DF: Grappa Blotto + Dor CL: Maxim Gorki Theater Germany 1997

1. D: Trogisch / Gebin DF: Grappa Blotto + Dor CL: Maxim Gorki Theater   Germany 1996 - 98

PANTONE 327 U   PANTONE 302 U
PANTONE Process Black U   PANTONE Process Black U

2. D: Trogisch DF: Grappa Blotto + Dor CL: Maxim Gorki Theater   Germany 1997

PANTONE 320 U   PANTONE 1805 U
PANTONE Process Black U   PANTONE Process Black U

PANTONE Process Black U | 1. D, P: MBrunner   DF: büro destruct vs Weltschmertz   CL: Dampfzentrale Bern   Switzerland   1997

PANTONE Process Black C
PANTONE 124 C | 2. D: MBrunner   DF: büro destruct   CL: Dampfzentrale Bern   Switzerland   1997

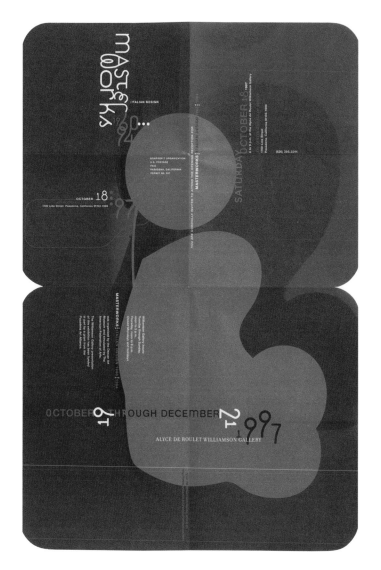

1. CD: Stuart I. Frolick AD: Denise Gonzales Crisp D: Caral Figueroa DF: Art Center College of Design - Design Office CL: Art Center College of Design
USA 1997

PANTONE 172 U
PANTONE Black 4 U 2X

2. CD, AD, D: Hajdeja S. Ehline DF: Super Natural Design CL: Southern Exposure Gallery   USA 1995

PANTONE 447 U

EARLY MUSIC Wir müssen die Vergangenheit erfinden, die Zukunft neu gestalten. Dies beides bringt die Gegenwart hervor. Entdeckung endet nie. *John Cage* Early Music zeigt das Kronos Quartet von seiner meditativen Seite. In sensibler Weise hat Kronos hier erstmals ein durchgehendes Programm mit Werken zusammengestellt, die nahezu 1200 Jahre Kompositionsgeschichte umfassen. Angefangen bei den griechischen

KRONOS QUARTET Das Kronos Quartet aus San Fran hat mit einem klassischen Streichquartett gerade noch das Instrument und die Sitzordnung gemeinsam. David Harrington gründete diese auwöhnliche Formation 1973 in Seattle. Das Quartett spielt seit der Übelung nach San Francisco im Jahre 1977 in seiner jetzigen Besetzungständig wachsende Repertoire des Kronos Quartet gehört fast ausslich dem 20. Jahrhundert an. Zwar greift Kronos bisweilen auf modernsiker wie Alban Berg, Bela Bartók und Charles Ives zurück; fast die Hälfgespielten Musik entstand jedoch eigens für das Kronos Quartet und in engem Kontakt zu lebenden Meistern wie Steve Reich, John Zorn, Mikolaj Górecki und Terry Riley sowie mit vielen avantgardistischen jKomponisten entwickelt. Bei der Auswahl der Partituren öffnet sicQuartett gern neuen Strömungen und Experimenten, wagt nicht selten

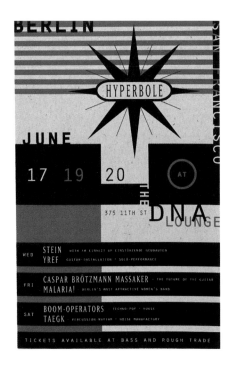

PANTONE Process Black U
PANTONE 173 U
1. D, P, CW, DF: Cyan CL: Freunde Guter Musik e. v. Germany 1998

PANTONE Process Black U
PANTONE 1797 U
2. CD, AD, D: Christie Rixford DF: Super Natural Design CL: DNA Lounee USA 1996

1. AD, D, P: Heather Heflin P: Kurt Smith CW: Jane Buckman DF: Cornish College of the Arts, Publications Dept.
CL: Cornish College of the Arts   USA 1997

PANTONE 185 U
PANTONE Process Black U

2. CD, AD, D: Herbert Rohsiepe CL: Rohsiepe Graphische Formgebung   Germany 1997

PANTONE 877 U

3. CD, AD, D: Herbert Rohsiepe DF: Rohsiepe Graphische Formgebung CL: KGB Music Agency   Germany 1998

PANTONE 877 U
PANTONE 1925 U

PANTONE 133 U
PANTONE 4535 U

PANTONE 618 U
PANTONE 385 U

 1, AD, D: Akira Sumi DF: Antenna Graphic Base CL: Maki Hiroshige Atelier Co. , Ltd. Japan 1998

PANTONE Process Black U

 2. CD, AD, D: John Ball D: Deborah Hom DF: Mires Design, Inc. CL: California Center for the Arts Museum USA 1995

PEACE ON EARTH

COME DISTURB IT WITH US

JANUARY 6TH, 1996, AT THE FINEST PARTY ON

EARTH

...HAD AT ... WE'VE GOT NEW DIGS, A NEW YEAR AND A WHOLE NEW BATCH OF RESOLUTIONS JUST WAIT-ING TO BE BROKEN. NOT TO MENTION A LIVE BAND AND GUESTS TO MATCH. SO JOIN US AT OUR NEW LOCALE [605 WILLIAMSON STREET] ON JANUARY 6TH FROM 8 P.M. TO MIDNIGHT.

PLANET DESIGN COMPANY
605 WILLIAMSON STREET
MADISON, WISCONSIN 53703

CALL 605.256.0000 IF YOU NEED MORE INFORMATION

-PARK & ENTER ON THE LAKE SIDE OF THE BUILDING-

DF, CL: Planet Design Co.   USA 1995

PANTONE 377 U
PANTONE 177 U

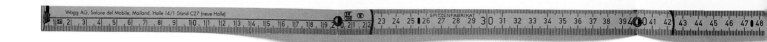

Salone del Mobile, Milano

Wir freuen uns auf Ihren Besuch an unserem Stand anlässlich der Möbelmesse in Mailand vom 16. bis 21. April 1998, von 9.30 bis 18.30 Uhr, Halle 14/1 Stand C27

Wogg AG, Im Grund 16, CH-5405 Baden, Telefon +41.56.493 38 21, Telefax +41.56.493 40 87

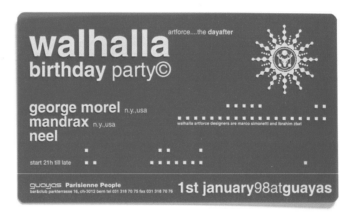

| | PANTONE Process Black U
PANTONE 877 U | 1. CD: Achim Heine / Michael Lenz / Peter Zizka AD: Sonía Reck CL: Wogg   Germany 1998 |

| | PANTONE 877 C | White | PANTONE Process Black C | 2. D: Marco Simonetti / Ibrahim Zbat DF: Walhalla Artforce CL: Guayas Club Switzerland 1998 |

| | PANTONE 804 U
PANTONE 877 U | 3. D: Claudia Meythaler DF, CL: 9D   Switzerland 1997 |

Salone del Mobile, Milano

Nous nous réjouissons de votre visite sur notre stand lors du *Salon du meuble à Milan* du 16 au 21 avril 1998, 9 h 30 à 18 h 30, Pavillon 14/1 Stand C27

Wogg AG, Im Grund 16, CH-5405 Baden, Telefon + 41.56.493 38 21, Telefax + 41.56.493 40 87

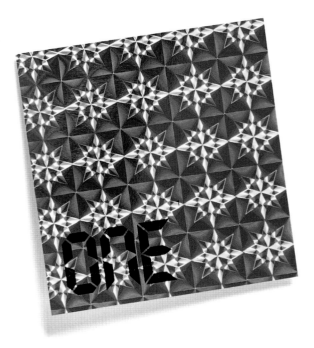

4. AD, D: Ron Faas / Tirso Francés P, DF: Dietwee CL: MIC   Netherlands 1997

PANTONE 877 C
PANTONE 1817 C

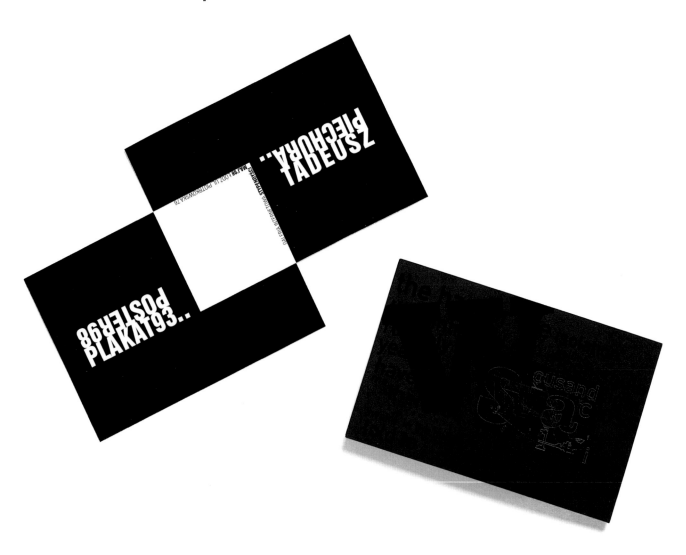

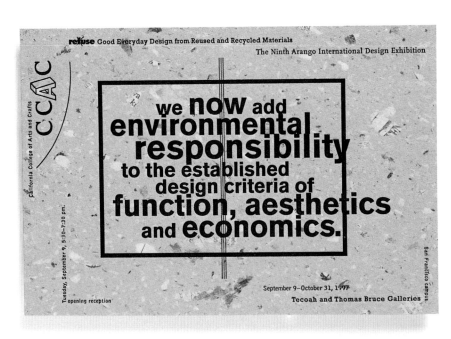

PANTONE Process Black U | 1. CD, AD, D, CW: Tadeusz Piechura CW: Wojciech Wycichowski DF: Atelier Tadeusz Piechura CL: Galeria Internetowa "Stypendysci"   Poland 1998

PANTONE 4515 C
PANTONE 5395 C | 2. CD, AD, D: Justin Greenleaf DF: Soliton Wave CL: Costume National   Italy 1998

H   PANTONE Process Black U | 3. AD, D: Bob Aufuldish DF: Aufuldish & Warinner CL: California College of Arts and Crafts, Oliver Art Center   USA 1997

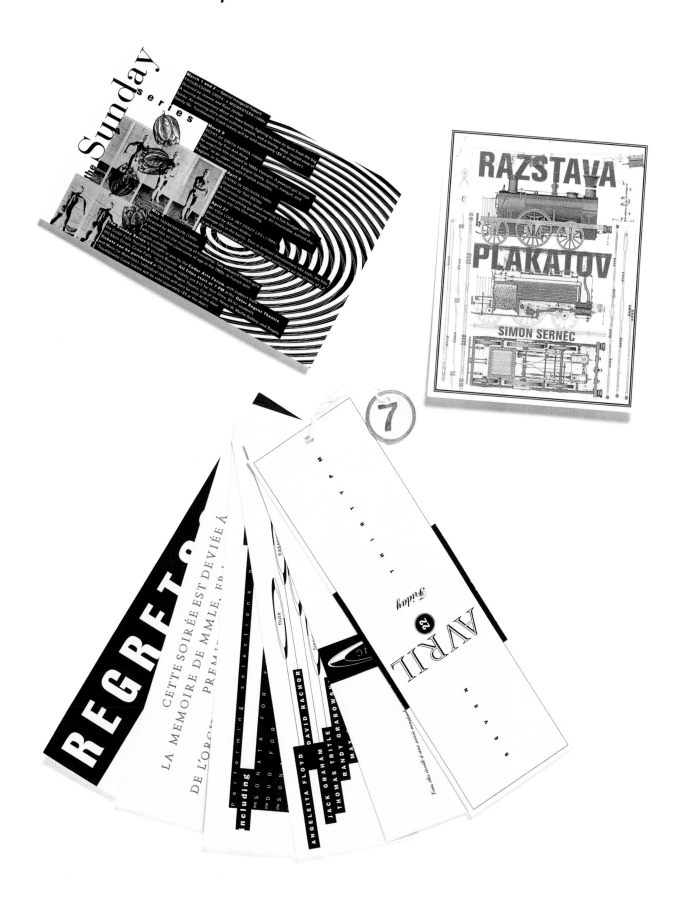

1. CD, AD, D: Philip Fass CW: Bettina Fabos CL: Cedar Arts Forum   USA 1997 | PANTONE Process Black C | ▮

2. AD, D: Simon Sernec DF: Decity & SS Creation CL: Culturac Center Zidanimost   Slovenia 1997 | PANTONE Process Black C / PANTONE 185 C | ▮▮

3. CD, AD, D, CW: Philip Fass CL: Harvey Hess   USA 1995 | PANTONE Process Black U | ▮

PANTONE Red 032 U
PANTONE 285 U

PANTONE 390 U
PANTONE Process Black U

D: Thomas Bruggisser DF: Grafiktraktor CL: Bruggisser Thomas   Switzerland 1998

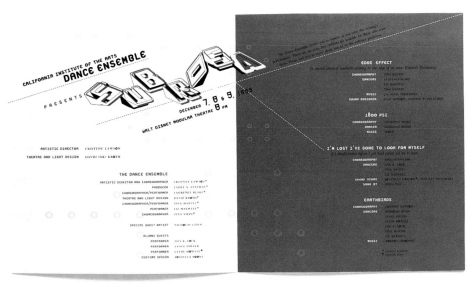

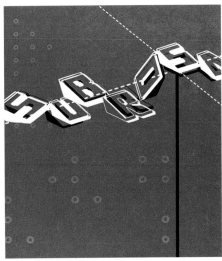

1. D: Jennifer Moody DF: California Institute of the Arts, Office of Public Affairs CL: California Institute of the Arts, School of Dance   USA 1995

PANTONE 207 U	
PANTONE 282 U	

2. CD: Stuart I. Frolick AD: Denise Gonzales Crisp D: Carla Figueroa DF: Art Center College of Design - Design Office CL: Art Center College of Design
USA 1998

PANTONE 180 U	
PANTONE Warm Red U	

85

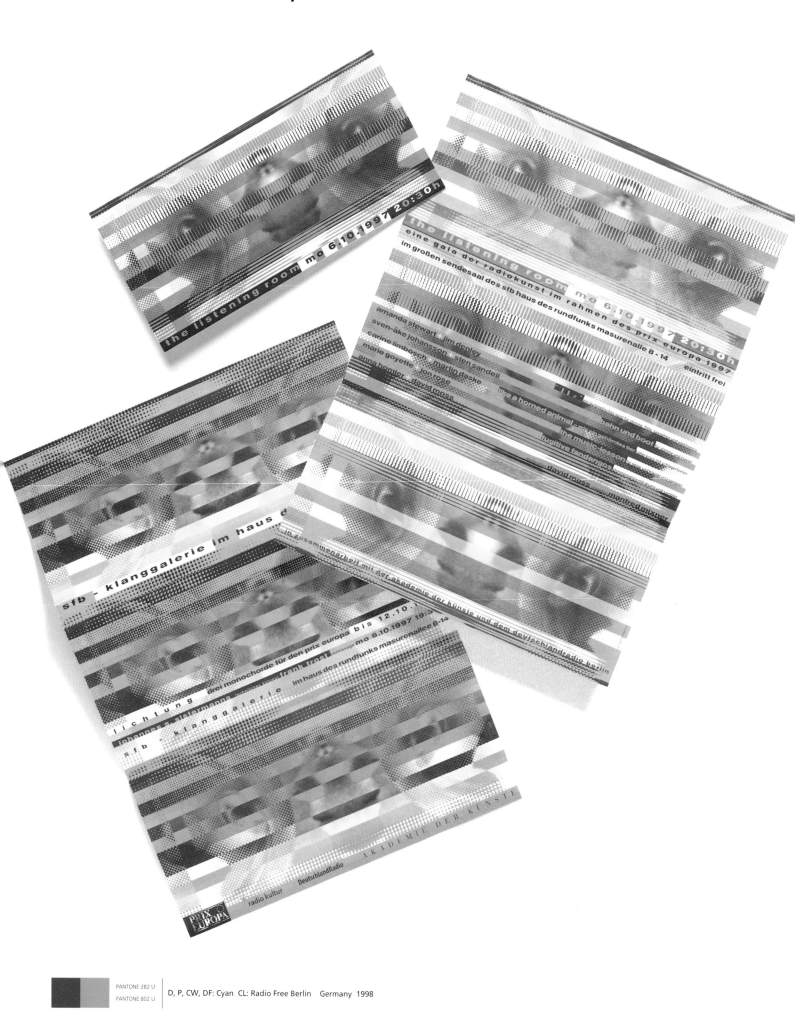

PANTONE 282 U
PANTONE 802 U

D, P, CW, DF: Cyan   CL: Radio Free Berlin   Germany 1998

1. AD: Mark D: Takashi Ishide DF: Graphicmart CL: Papier Luna   Japan 1998

PANTONE 300 U
PANTONE 326 U

PANTONE 1375 U
PANTONE 122 U

PANTONE 268 U
PANTONE 2736 U

2. CD, AD, D: Takeshi Nishimura DF: Completo Inc. CL: Tomorrowland Co. , Ltd.   Japan 1997

PANTONE 357 U
PANTONE Process Black U

3. CD: Shigeo Endo AD, D: Shintaro Miwa DF: 3 O Graphics CL: e - street bagels, Inc.   Japan 1998

PANTONE 116 U
PANTONE 2738 U

PANTONE 116 C
PANTONE 295 C

CD: School "Radeče" AD, D: Simon Sernec I: Primary School Pupils(11 - 14 years old) CW: School(Pupils) CL: Primary School "Radeče"   Slovenia 1997

1. CD, AD, D, I: Hugo Ender D: René Dalpra CW: Spielkreis Götzis CL: Spielkreis Götzis   Austria 1996

2. CD, AD, D: Julia Chong Tam CW: Jan Gonzales DF: Julia Tam Design CL: UCLA Conference Services   USA 1998

Energie aus Biogas
Das Förderprogramm
des Landes Vorarlberg

Warum Biogas?

Biogas ist ein erneuerbarer Energieträger.
Knappe Ressourcen wie Kohle, Erdöl und
Erdgas werden geschont.

Im Gegensatz zur offenen Gülle-Lagerung kann
das Methan in einer geschlossenen Biogas-
anlage nicht entweichen. Es wird zur Energie-
gewinnung genutzt statt die Atmosphäre
zu belasten.

Die vergorene Gülle ist reich an Stickstoff,
aber arm an Viren, Bakterien und Parasiten.
Ein idealer Dünger, der die Fruchtbarkeit
des Bodens und somit gesunde Pflanzen-
kulturen fordert.

Biogasgülle riecht kaum noch, ist homogener
und läßt sich leichter rühren, pumpen und ver-
teilen als im ursprünglichen Zustand.

Die Nutzung von Biogasgülle ist ein aktiver
Beitrag zur Kreislaufwirtschaft.

PANTONE Process Black U
PANTONE 116 U

PANTONE 123 U
PANTONE 361 U

AD, D : Sigi Ramoser CL: Lano Vorarlberg   Austria 1997 - 98

1. CD: Pattie Belle Hastings D: Bjorn Akselsen DF: Icehouse Design CL: Niki Paris   USA 1997

PANTONE 363 U
PANTONE 459 U

2. CD, AD, D: John Sayles CW: Kay Hyde DF: Sayles Graphic Design CL: Science Center of Iowa   USA 1998

PANTONE 158 U
PANTONE Reflex Blue U

PANTONE 872 U
PANTONE Black U

CD, AD, D, P, I: Scott Thares AD, I, CW: Anna Weber DF: Thares Design CL: Anna Webert & Scott Thares   USA 1997

Kindern ein Zuhause

Coccinelle, démoiselle,
bête à bon dieu,
cocci-
nelle, démoiselle,
vole jusqu'aux cieux.
Petit points blancs-
elle attend,
Petits points rouge-
elle bouge,
Petits points noirs-
Coccinelle,
au re-
voir

Marienkäfer klein,
Gottestierlein,
Marien-
käfer klein,
flieg zum Himmel hinauf.
Weiße Pünktchen-
er bleibt stehn,
rote Pünktchen-
will weitergehn,
schwarze Pünktchen-
Marienkäfer,
auf Wieder-
sehn!

SOS-Kinderdörfer

Wir haben am

On December 8th, 1997

8. Dezember 1997

Tom and Andrea

geheiratet,

were married.

Tom und Andrea.

1. CD, AD, D: Katrien Florin CL: Sofie & Steven Vanhoutte   Belgium 1997

PANTONE Process Black C
PANTONE 459 C

2. D: Kerstin Antony DF: Büro für gestaltung   Germany 1995

PANTONE Process Black C
PANTONE 186 C

3. CD, D, I: Thomas Ferraro D, I: Andrea CL: Andrea / Thomas Ferraro   USA 1998

PANTONE Process Black U
PANTONE 485 U

93

Our Master Tee is celebrating his
30th Century
Come and sink your teeth this 24th May
Ceremony begins at four hours before
the stroke of midnight
Search for his Castle at
Nine Chesilton Road SW6's 6.1

Butler may refuse entry to guest who
are not dress appropriately

Be warn that you come at
your on risk and may seriously
damage your health.

R.S.V.P 0171 610 6576

PANTONE Process Black C
Red Stamp Ink

CD, AD, D: Albert Kueh DF: @Ka CL: Fiona Harmer and Phil Tee   UK 1997

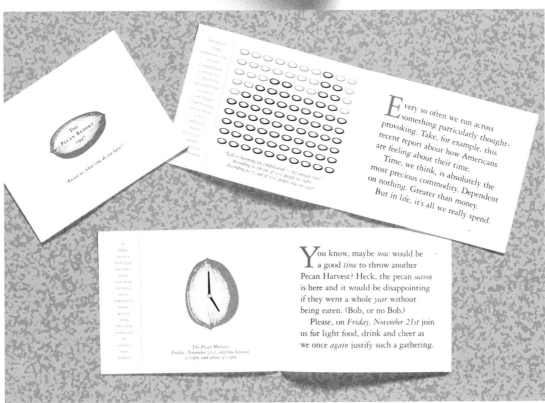

1. CD, CW: Mitsuko Shimura AD, D: Kisei Oka CL: Doms Architect's   Japan 1998

PANTONE 425 C
PANTONE 194 C

2. CD, AD, D, CW: Forrest Richardson DF, CL: Richardson or Richardson   USA 1997

PANTONE 499 U
PANTONE Process Black U

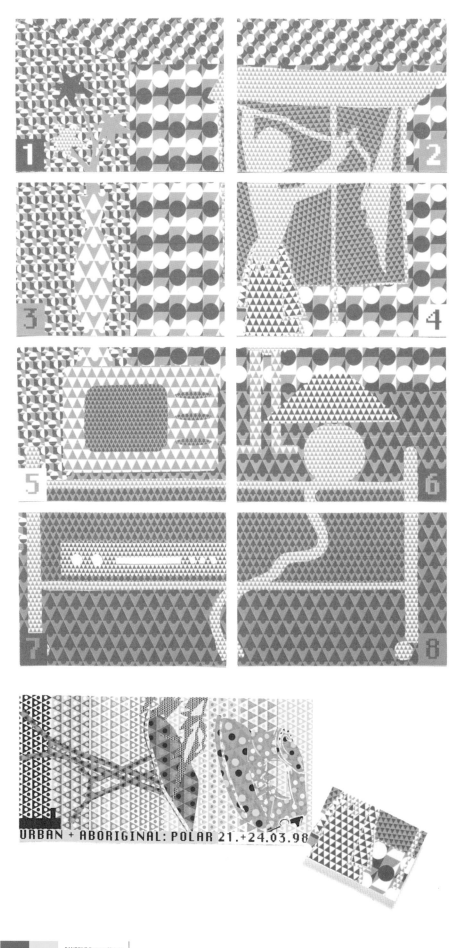

PANTONE 804 C
PANTONE 806 C

PANTONE Process Blue U
PANTONE Yellow U

D, P, CW, DF: Cyan CL: Freunde Guter Musik Berlin e. v. Germany 1998

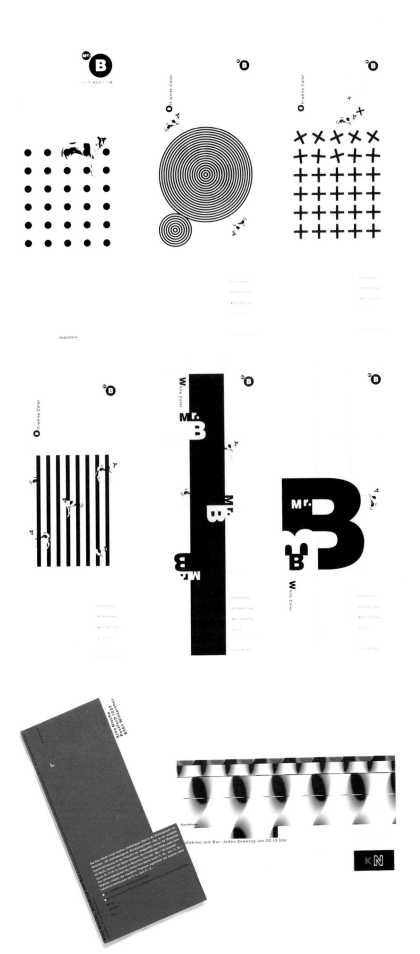

1. AD: Ken Miki D: Junji Osaki P: Kuninobu Fukuda DF: Ken Miki & Associates CL: Heiwa Paper   Japan 1996

PANTONE Process Black C
PANTONE Process Black U

2. D: Thomas Bruggisser DF: Grafiktraktor CL: Kino Nische   Switzerland 1998

PANTONE 186 C
PANTONE Process Black C

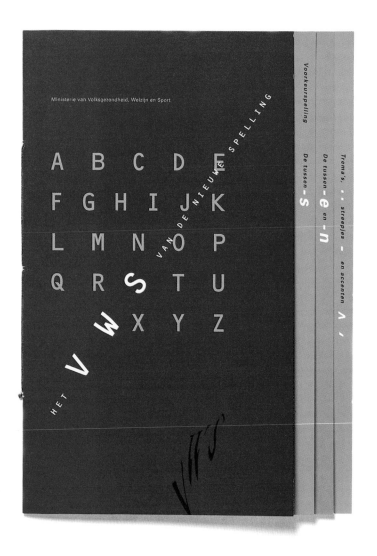

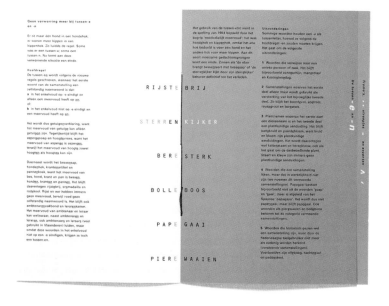

PANTONE Reflex Blue C
PANTONE 730 C

CD, AD, D: Ben Faydherbe   CW: Marcel Wiegman   DF: Faydherbe / De Vringer   CL: Ministry for Public Health, Welfare and Sports   Netherlands 1996

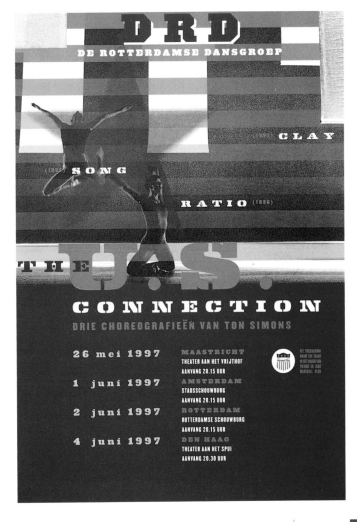

1. AD: Ron Faas / Tirso Francés   AD, D: Harmen Liemburg   P: ANP Picture   DF: Dietwee   CL: LOKV   Netherlands 1998

PANTONE 2935 C
PANTONE 1788 C

2. CD, AD, D: Wout de Vringer   P: Leo Van Velzen   DF: Faydherbe / De Vringer   CL: De Rotterdamse Dans Groep   Netherlands 1997

PANTONE Blue 072 U
PANTONE Red 032 U

PANTONE 123 U
PANTONE Process Black U

1. 2. CD, AD: Forrest Richardson D: Jesse von Glück I: Key Rash(1) CW: Forrest Richardson(1) DF: Richardson or Richardson CL: Access Laserpress
USA 1997

PANTONE 116 C
PANTONE 2627 C

3. D, P: Ebel Kuipers DF: Ebel Kuipers Grafisch Ontwerper CL: Jannie Strijk / Ebel Kuipers   Netherlands 1997

CD, AD, D, P, I, CW, DF: Fantastic New Designment GmbH CL: Deutsche Post Ag.   Germany 1998

PANTONE Process Black C

PANTONE 116 C

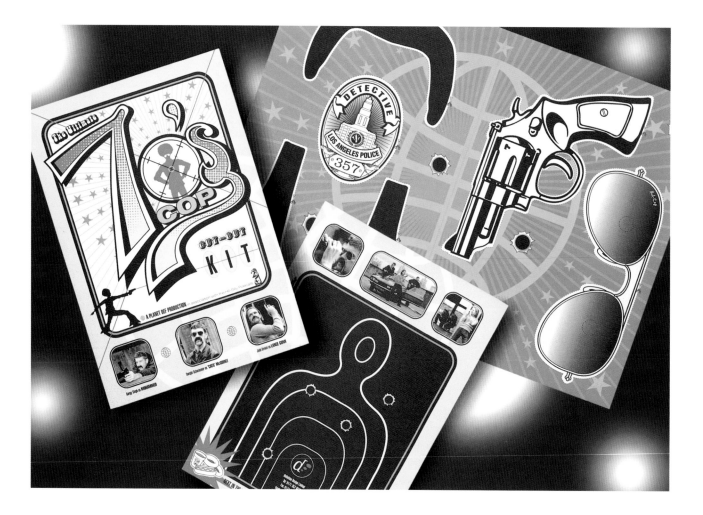

PANTONE Orange 021 C
PANTONE Black C

1. CD, AD, D: Neill Furmston D: Chris Waind DF: Definition Design Limited CL: Planet Def   UK 1998

PANTONE Process Blue C
PANTONE Process Black C

2. CD: Ichiro Hatakeyama AD: Naohiro Masuda D: Yasuhiro Kawahara I: Souta Hirao C: Noboru Inoue DF: Kokokusha Co. , Ltd.
CL: Hiroya International Co. , Ltd.   Japan 1998

PANTONE 1585 C
PANTONE Process Black C

3. CD, AD, D: Etsuko Kimura CL: Bran - New Made Co. , Ltd. Japan 1997

1. CD, AD, D, I: Michael Strassburger DF: Modern Dog CL: Chicken Soup Brigade   USA 1997

PANTONE 2975 C
PANTONE 1795 C

2. CD: Troy Bailly AD: Stephen Parkes I: David Papineau DF: Prototype Design CL: Poke in the Eye Productions   Canada 1997

PANTONE Process Black U
PANTONE 300 U

3. CD, AD, D, I: Ryan McGinness CW: Orange 9mm DF: Ryan McGinness Studio CL: NG Records   USA 1998

PANTONE Process Black C
PANTONE 2915 C

1

2

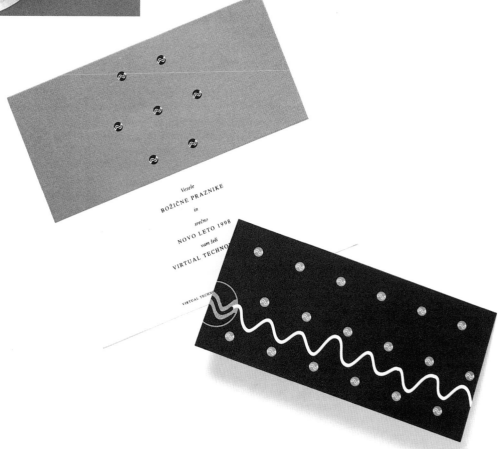

PANTONE 872 U
PANTONE 541 U

1. CD, AD, D, I: John Sayles CW: Kristin Lennert DF: Sayles Graphic Design CL: Allied Meats   USA 1997

PANTONE 280 U
PANTONE 874 U

2. AD, D, CW: Simon Sernec CL: Virtual Technologies   Slovenia 1997

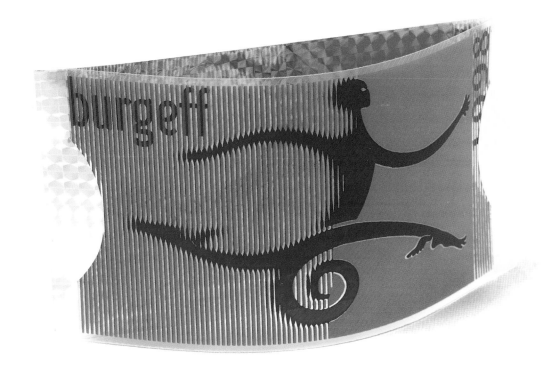

1. CD, D: Patrick Burgeff DF, CL: Burgeff Co.   Mexico 1997

PANTONE Warm Red U
PANTONE 286 C

2. AD, D: Simon Sernec I: Primary School Pupil (Laura Pukl 11 years old / Nina 11 years old) CW: School CL: Primary School(Radeče)   Slovenia 1997

PANTONE Reflex Blue C
PANTONE Yellow C

SPECIAL INGREDIENTS:
MSG - NO WAY

SATURDAY, MAY 31ST
AFTER TEN

DJ CLARENCE & FRIENDS
ZERO COVER - YOU NO PAY!

"FRED SAY YOU SUPER RUCKY"
POKEY IN THE EYE PARTY PRODUCT PERFECT
Made In Protoland

1. CD: Troy Bailly AD: Stephen Parkes I: David Papineau DF: Prototype Design CL: Poke in the Eye Productions   Canada 1997 | PANTONE Red 032 U

2. CD, AD, D: Hajdeja S. Ehline DF: Super Natural Design CL: Southern Exposure Gallery   USA 1995 | PANTONE Reflex Blue C

CD, AD, D: Harumi Kirima D: Fumitaka Yukawa DF: Kirima Design Office CL: Pia Corporation   Japan 1996

PANTONE 802 U
PANTONE Process Black U
PANTONE 806 U
PANTONE 804 U
PANTONE Process Black U
PANTONE 810 U
PANTONE Process Black U
PANTONE 802 U

AD, D: Bob Aufuldish I: John Hersey / Various Dingbat Fonts DF: Aufuldish & Warinner CL: California College of Arts and Crafts, Office of Enrollment Services   USA 1996

1

2

PANTONE 381 U
PANTONE Process Black U

PANTONE 122 U
PANTONE Process Black U

PANTONE 1505 U
PANTONE Process Black U

PANTONE 271 U
PANTONE Process Black U

1, AD, D: Masayuki Uchida DF: Voltage Co. , Ltd.
CL: Laforet Harajuku   Japan 1995

PANTONE 877 C
PANTONE Process Black C

2. CD, AD, D: Albert Kueh DF: @Ka CL: Gilbert Kueh and Felicity Angking   UK 1996

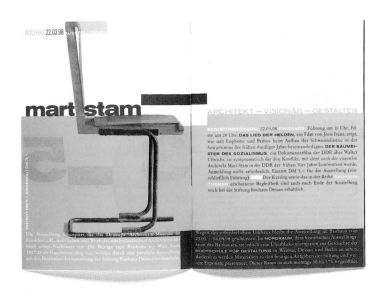

D, P, CW, DF: Cyan CL: Bauhaus Dessau Foundation   Germany 1998

| PANTONE 5115 U | | PANTONE 533 U | |
| PANTONE 544 U | | PANTONE 374 U | |

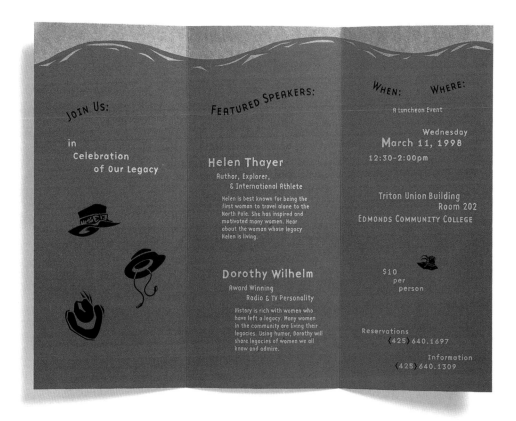

PANTONE 369 U   1. CD, AD, D: Thomas Neeser / Thomas Müller   DF: Neeser + Müller   CL: Marlis Kaulich   Switzerland   1998

PANTONE 8401 C
PANTONE Process Black C   2. CD: Patricia Belyea   D, I: Johnine Mac   DF: Belyea Design Alliance   CL: Stevens Healthcare   USA   1998

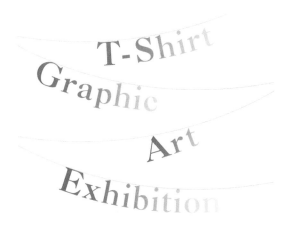

1. CD, AD, D: Junko Hayashi DF: Bros Co. , Ltd. CL: Dress Mode Kazumi   Japan 1998   PANTONE 2635 C / PANTONE 150 C

2. AD: Katsumi Komagata D: Aki Ishijima DF: One Stroke Co. , Ltd. CL: F. D. C. Products Inc.   Japan 1998   PANTONE 877 C

3. AD, D: Shigehisa Takenaga DF: Takenaga Design Office CL: JAGDA   Japan 1998   PANTONE 339 U / PANTONE 286 U

PANTONE 374 U
PANTONE 285 U

1. CL: Kid Blue Co., Ltd.   Japan 1998

PANTONE 8220 C
PANTONE Process Black C

2. CD, AD, D: Takeshi Nishimura DF: Completo Inc. CL: Tomorrowland Co., Ltd.   Japan 1997

3. 4. 5. CD: Naruhito Takayanagi AD: Shoko Takayanagi D: Miho Higashi DF: Christmas
Design Room CL: Bellmode Co., Ltd.   Japan 1996-98

6. D: Kyoko Nakazawa CL: Kid Blue Co., Ltd.   Japan 1997

PANTONE Process Black U
PANTONE Process Blue U

1. AD, D: Tirso Francés / Dylan Fracareta DF: Dietwee CL: Wink Party Artwork   Netherlands 1997

PANTONE Process Black C
PANTONE 873 C

2. CD: Anja Osterwalder AD: Oliver Krimmel D: Thorsten Klöpfer DF: I - D Büro GmbH CL: Pauls Boutique   Germany 1997

PANTONE 187 U   PANTONE 370 U
PANTONE 280 U   PANTONE 280 U

3. D: Dylan Fracareta DF: Dietwee CL: Wink Party Artwork / Club de Ville   Netherlands 1997

1. D, CW: Makiko Kobayashi CL: Space Lab Yellow   Japan 1998

PANTONE 809 C
PANTONE Process Black C

2. D, I: H1reber DF: büro destruct CL: Reitschule Bern   Switzerland 1998

PANTONE 5395 C
PANTONE 8202 C

3. D: H1reber DF: büro destruct CL: Reitschule Bern   Switzerland 1998

PANTONE 5483 U
PANTONE Process Black U

D, CW: Makiko Kobayashi CL: Space Lab Yellow   Japan 1997-98

PANTONE 1807 C
PANTONE 374 C

PANTONE 201 U
PANTONE 375 U

CD, D: Ron Faas / Harmen Liemburg D: Dylan Fracareta P: ANP Picture DF: Dietwee CL: LOKV   Netherlands 1997

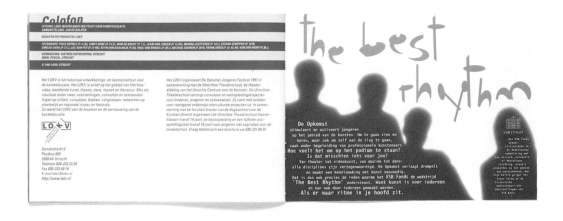

PANTONE 201 U
PANTONE 375 U

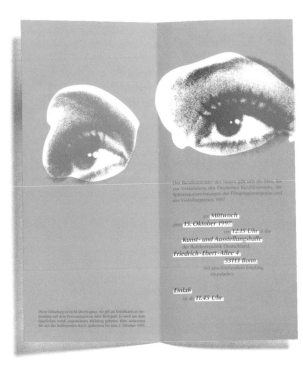

1997

Deutscher Kurzfilmpreis

Filmprogrammpreise

Verleiherpreis

des Bundesministers des Innern

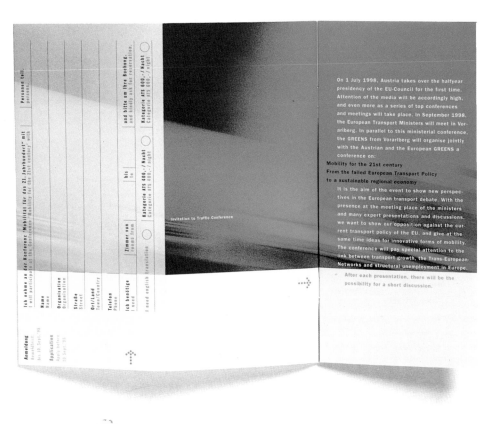

From the failed European
Transport Policy to a sustainable
regional economy
Invitation to the Green Traffic Conference
13 - 15 September 1998
in Feldkirch/Austria, Pförtnerhaus

Verkehr   trafic

traffic

traffico

Mobility for the 21st century

On 1 July 1998, Austria takes over the halfyear
presidency of the EU-Council for the first time.
Attention of the media will be accordingly high,
and even more as a series of top conferences
and meetings will take place. In September 1998,
the European Transport Ministers will meet in Vorarlberg. In parallel to this ministerial conference,
the GREENS from Vorarlberg will organise jointly
with the Austrian and the European GREENS a
conference on:
Mobility for the 21st century
From the failed European Transport Policy
to a sustainable regional economy
It is the aim of the event to show new perspec-
tives in the European transport debate. With the
presence at the meeting place of the ministers
and many expert presentations and discussions,
we want to show our opposition against the current transport policy of the EU, and give at the
same time ideas for innovative forms of mobility.
The conference will pay special attention to the
link between transport growth, the Trans-European-
Networks and structural unemployment in Europe.
After each presentation, there will be the
possibility for a short discussion.

PANTONE 8483 C
PANTONE 802 C

1. CD, AD, D, P, I, CW, DF: Fantastic New Designment GmbH   CL: Forum Film GmbH   Germany 1997

PANTONE Process Black U
PANTONE 802 U

2. CD, D: Peter Felder D: Martin Wieland CW: Johannes Rauch / Katharina Wiesflecker DF: Felder Grafikdesign CL: Die Grünen, Die Grüne
Bildungswerkstatt, Greens in the European Parliament   Austria 1998

the**procrastination**solution

new**members**

aigamnjan

janca**l**e**nd**er

1. CD: Steven Sikora AD, D: Tom Riddle P: Michael Crouser DF: Design Guys CL: AIGA Minnesota   USA 1998

PANTONE 5615 C
PANTONE 383 C

2. D: Kees Wagenaars DF: Case CL: Boxtheater   Netherlands 1998

PANTONE Process Black U
PANTONE 389 U

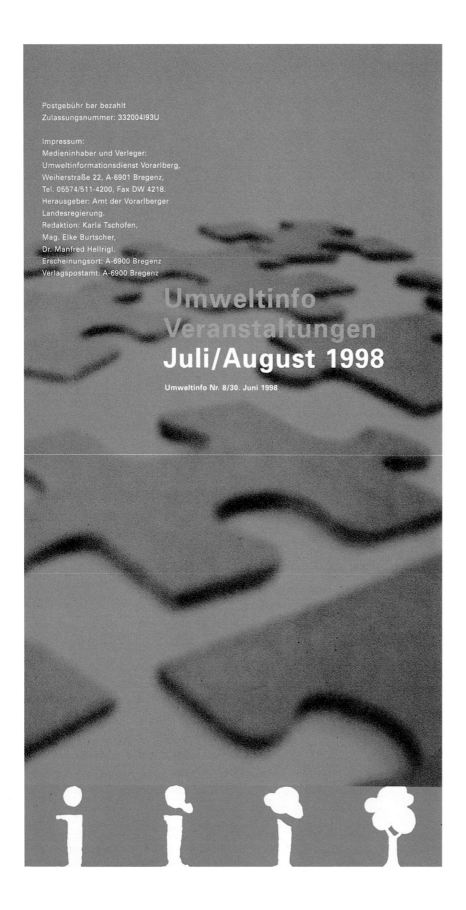

Postgebühr bar bezahlt
Zulassungsnummer: 332004I93U

Impressum:
Medieninhaber und Verleger:
Umweltinformationsdienst Vorarlberg,
Weiherstraße 22, A-6901 Bregenz,
Tel. 05574/511-4200, Fax DW 4218.
Herausgeber: Amt der Vorarlberger
Landesregierung.
Redaktion: Karla Tschofen,
Mag. Elke Burtscher,
Dr. Manfred Hellrigl.
Erscheinungsort: A-6900 Bregenz
Verlagspostamt: A-6900 Bregenz

Umweltinfo
Veranstaltungen
Juli/August 1998

Umweltinfo Nr. 8/30. Juni 1998

Umweltinfo
Veranstaltungen
Juni 1998

Umweltinfo Nr. 7/29. Mai 1998

Umweltinfo
Veranstaltungen
April 1998

Umweltinfo Nr. 4/31. März 1998

PANTONE Process Black U
PANTONE 321 U

AD, D: Sigi Ramoser / Klaus Österle CL: Umwelt Informations Oienst   Austria 1997-98

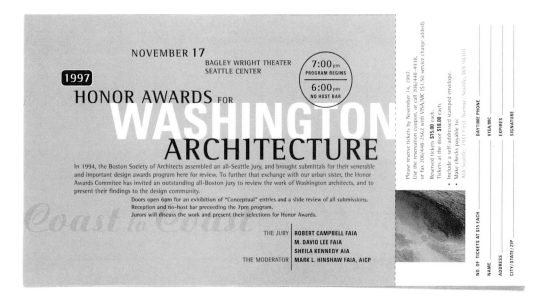

CD, D: Amy Lam D: Brent Whiting DF: NBBJ Graphic Design CL: AIA Seattle USA 1997

PANTONE Process Black U

PANTONE 3125 U

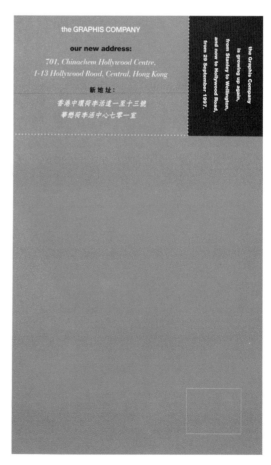

the GRAPHIS COMPANY

our new address:

701, Chinachem Hollywood Centre,
1-13 Hollywood Road, Central, Hong Kong

新地址：

香港中環荷李活道一至十三號
華懋荷李活中心七零一室

the Graphis Company
is growing up again,
from Stanley to Wellington,
and now to Hollywood Road,
from 29 September 1997.

PANTONE 4545 C
PANTONE Process Black C

1. CD: Takako Terunuma AD, D: Akihiko Tsukamoto DF: Accompany Co. , Ltd. CL: Tokyo Design Center   Japan 1996

PANTONE Orange 021 C
PANTONE 412 C

2. CD, AD: Bon Kwan D, P: Wicky Lam DF, CL: The Graphis Co., Ltd.   China 1997

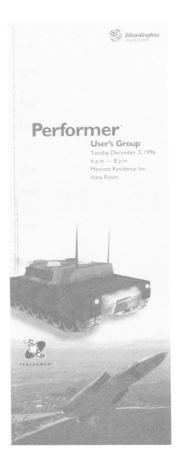

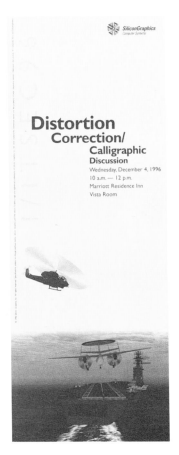

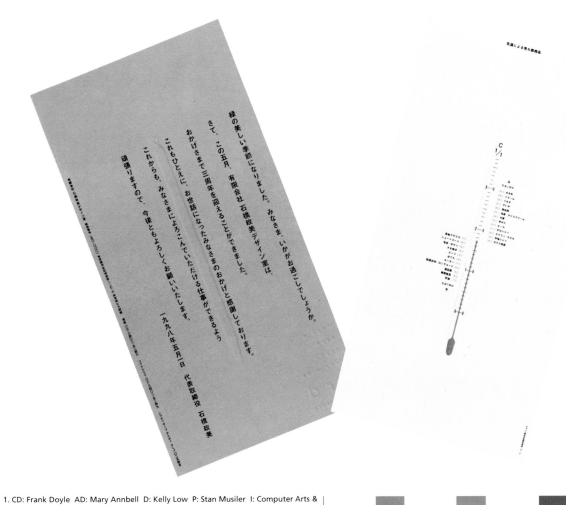

1. CD: Frank Doyle AD: Mary Annbell D: Kelly Low P: Stan Musiler I: Computer Arts & Development; Coryphaevs; Paramom Simulation, Inc. DF: Silicon Graphics / Corporate Communications, Creative Dept. CL: Silicon Graphics, Inc.   USA 1996

2. AD, D: Masami Ishibashi C: Masakazu Nifuji DF, CL: Masami Ishibashi Design Inc.   Japan 1998

PANTONE 449 U   PANTONE 582 U   PANTONE 289 U   PANTONE 167 U

PANTONE 361 U
PANTONE Process Black U

PANTONE 1797 U
PANTONE Process Black U

printed material

	PANTONE 1787 C		PANTONE 102 C		PANTONE 8041 C		PANTONE 169 C		PANTONE 5493 C
	PANTONE 293 C		PANTONE 282 C		PANTONE 282 C		PANTONE 5275 C		PANTONE 228 C

D, I, CW: Makiko Kobayashi CL: Space Lab Yellow   Japan 1997-98

1. AD: Mark D: Takashi Ishide DF: Graphicmart CL: Nite Cafe Qoo   Japan 1997 - 98

| PANTONE 8081 C | | PANTONE Process Black C | | PANTONE 871 C | |
| PANTONE 1625 C | | PANTONE 877 C | | PANTONE Warm Red C | |

2. D: Walter Stähli / Marco Simonetti / Ibrahim Zbat DF: Walhalla Artforce CL: Exkandalo   Switzerland 1998

| PANTONE Process Black C | | PANTONE Process Black C | |
| PANTONE 876 C | | PANTONE 805 C | |

PANTONE Process Black C
PANTONE 804 C

1. CD, AD, D: J. J. F. G. Borrenbergs / R. Verkaart DF: Stoere Binken Design CL: Sirius   Netherlands 1998

PANTONE Process Black C
PANTONE 8341 C

2. D,CW: Makiko Kobayashi CL: Space Lab Yellow   Japan 1998

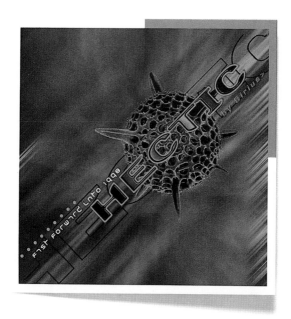

1. CD, AD, D: J. J. F. G. Borrenbergs DF: Stoere Binken Design CL: Sirius   Netherlands 1998

PANTONE 3302 C
PANTONE Red 032 C

2. CD, AD, D: J. J. F. G. Borrenbergs / R.Verkaart DF: Stoere Binken Design CL: Sirius   Netherlands 1998

PANTONE 2747 C
PANTONE 376 C

PANTONE 871 C
PANTONE Process Black C

PANTONE 805 C
PANTONE Process Black C

D: Ibrahim Zbat / Marco Simonetti / Walter Stähli P: Walhalla - Team DF: Walhalla Artforce   Switzerland 1998

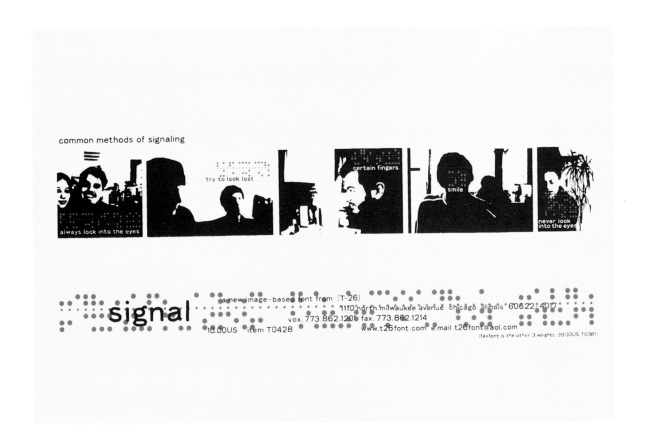

1. CD, AD, D: Carlos Segura D: Susana Detembleque DF: Segura Inc. CL: [T-26] Digital Type Foundry   USA
1998

| PANTONE Process Black C |
| PANTONE Warm Red C |

2. CD, AD, D: Neill Furmston DF: Definition Design Limited CL: Xtravaganza Recordings   UK 1998

| PANTONE Black C | PANTONE Black C | PANTONE Black C |
| PANTONE 382 C | PANTONE 811 C | PANTONE 246 C |

1 2
3

PANTONE 5787 C
PANTONE 387 C

PANTONE Process Black C
PANTONE 723 C

PANTONE Process Black C
PANTONE 877 C

CD, AD, D: Oliver Krimmel (1. 2) / Anja Osterwalder (3) DF: I - D Büro GmbH
CL: Pauls Boutique   Germany 1997

1. D: Lopetz I: H1reber DF: büro destruct CL: Rote Fabrik Zürich   Switzerland 1997

PANTONE 2715 U
PANTONE 395 U

2. D, I: Lopetz DF: büro destruct CL: Reitschule Bern / Rote Fabrik Zürich   Switzerland 1997

PANTONE 301 U
PANTONE Warm Red U

3. 4. D: Lopetz DF: büro destruct CL: Reitschule Bern   Switzerland 1998

PANTONE 1797 C   PANTONE Orange 021 U
PANTONE 4525 C   PANTONE 357 U

loss and grieving

HELPING A FRIEND
THROUGH DIFFICULT TIMES

Last acts

helping

A FRIEND

through difficult times

When a friend is going through the process of losing a loved one, listening is as important as asking questions. When a person is grieving, others are often unsure of the "right" thing to say or do, and end up doing nothing. The following tips are designed to help you help a grieving person.

Last acts

loss and grieving

We don't know the right thing

to do or say... turning away

from reminders of death...

isolating loved ones who need

our presence.

~

IRA BYOCK, M.D.
AUTHOR OF DYING WELL

loss and grieving

HELPING CAREGIVERS
THROUGH DIFFICULT TIMES

Last acts

helping

CAREGIVERS

through difficult times

Caregiving is isolating. And the isolation doesn't end when caregiving is over. Each time a loved one becomes more ill, loses abilities, or isn't functioning on the same level as before, the grieving begins anew. The eventual death of the loved one brings a new round of grief that has different qualities because of the finality of the loss and the end of the important role as caregiver. If you want to help a caregiver or former caregiver, here are some suggestions.

Last acts
http://www.lastacts.org

loss and grieving

It is possible that nobody knows

about their situation, or that

friends and family simply stay

away because they don't know

what to do or how to help.

~

ROSALYNN CARTER
AUTHOR OF HELPING YOURSELF HELP
OTHERS, A BOOK FOR CAREGIVERS

| | PANTONE 610 U | | PANTONE 520 U | | PANTONE 625 U | | PANTONE 160 U |
| PANTONE Process Black U | | PANTONE Process Black U | | PANTONE Process Black U | | PANTONE Process Black U |

loss and grieving

HELPING THE ELDERLY
THROUGH DIFFICULT TIMES

Last acts.

helping

THE ELDERLY

through difficult times

Use family occasions in a positive way, by talking to those you care for about the end of life. Gather information about advance directives, living wills and health care proxies. Find books or other popular media to share with those you love in order to begin a dialogue about difficult issues. Use the following suggestions to help an older person through a difficult dying experience.

Last acts.

loss and grieving

I have felt with increasing ease,

that now familiar feeling of loss

and sorrow, and yet that comfort,

acceptance, at home with death.

I have lost my terror and denial

of death. I can live with its reality.

~

BETTY FRIEDAN
AUTHOR OF THE FOUNTAIN OF AGE

loss and grieving

ADVICE FOR HEALTH CARE PROVIDERS
CARING FOR DYING PATIENTS

Last acts.

helping

HEALTH CARE PROVIDERS

through difficult times

Following are some tips to help physicians discuss end-of-life issues with their patients. These tips have been endorsed by consumer organizations with respect for the physician-patient relationship and understanding that there may be variations of "tips" based on individual circumstances.

Last acts.

loss and grieving

...if peace and dignity are what we

delude ourselves to expect, most

of us will die wondering what we,

or our doctors, have done wrong.

~

SHERWIN NULAND, M.D.
AUTHOR OF HOW WE DIE

CD: Deborah Howard AD, D: Maggie Soldano D: Carolyn Bucy P: FPG Stock Photography DF: The Deborah Howard Agency, Ltd. CL: Barksdale Ballard   USA 1998

PANTONE 130 U
PANTONE 222 U

1. 2. D: Rod Tilley / Riko Tagashira P: Tony Cordoza DF: Kaiser McEuen, Inc. CL: California Mart USA 1997

PANTONE 275 U
PANTONE 5615 U

3. D: Riko Tagashira P: Suza Scalora DF: Kaiser McEuen, Inc. CL: California Mart USA 1998

PANTONE 1255 U
PANTONE 690 U

4. D: Riko Tagashira P: David Stewart / Toshio Nakajima DF: Kaiser McEuen, Inc. CL: California Mart USA 1998

1. CD: Patricia Belyea D: Naomi Murphy P: Jim Linna CW: Elizabeth E. Holland DF: Belyea Design Alliance CL: Stevens Hospital   USA 1998

PANTONE 8003 C
PANTONE 520 C

2. CD, AD, D: Catharine Bradbury CW, CL: Dunlop Art Gallery   Canada 1998

PANTONE 274 C
PANTONE 384 C

PANTONE 2728 U
PANTONE 166 U

CD, AD, D, CW: Ilja Sallacz CL: Thomas + Renate Rossmann   Germany 1997

1. CD: David Papineau AD: Troy Bailly D: Stephen Parkes DF: Prototype Design CL: Red Lounge Nightclub   Canada 1998

PANTONE Process Black C
PANTONE 8883 C

2. D: Kees Wagenaars DF: Case CL: Teater '77   Netherlands 1997

PANTONE Red 032 U
PANTONE 252 U

3. CD, AD, D, P, DF: André M. Baldinger CL: Companie Le Crochet à Nuages   Switzerland 1997

PANTONE Process Black C
PANTONE 2727 C

PANTONE 1525 U
PANTONE 5115 U

D: Susanne Schropp DF: Diva Design CL: Teachers College, Columbia University   USA 1997

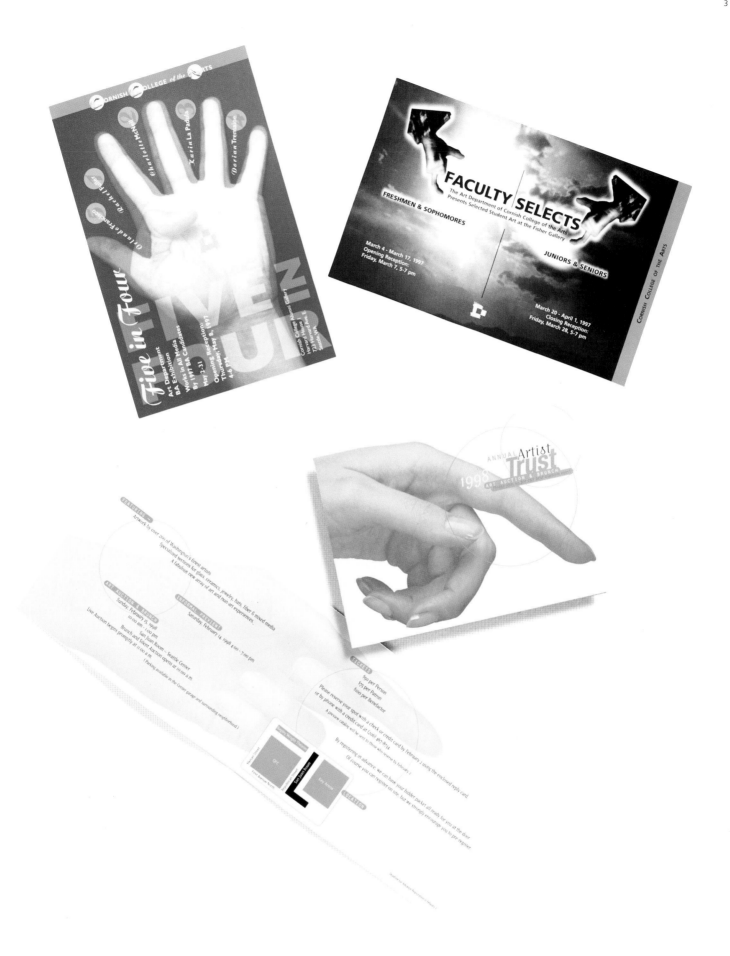

1. 2. AD, D, P: Heather Heflin DF: Cornish College of the Arts, Publications Dept. CL: Cornish College of the Arts   USA 1997

PANTONE 377 C
PANTONE 219 C
PANTONE 297 C
PANTONE Process Black C

3. D: Roddy Grant DF: NBBJ Graphic Design CL: Artist Trust   USA 1998

PANTONE 8363 C
PANTONE Black C

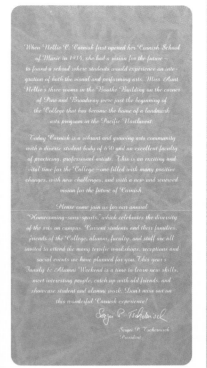

PANTONE 144 U
PANTONE 3415 U

AD, D, P: Heather Heflin   CW: Andy Gary   DF: Cornish College of the Arts, Publications Dept.   CL: Cornish College of the Arts   USA 1997

1. AD, D: Kathy Warinner DF: Aufuldish & Warinner CL: Dancer's Group / Footwork / Mercy Sidbury   USA 1995

PANTONE Process Black C
PANTONE Process Blue C

2. AD, D, Dingbat D, P: Bob Aufuldish DF: Aufuldish & Warinner CL: California College of Arts and Crafts, Office of Development   USA 1997

PANTONE Process Black U
PANTONE Process Blue U

3. AD, D, P: Bob Aufuldish P: Eric Heiman DF: Aufuldish & Warinner CL: California College of Arts and Crafts, Office of Enrollment Services   USA 1996

PANTONE Process Black U

Jessica Dodge
Femmes
Nancy Morrow
Fatales
Liza vonRosenstiel

Jena Scott

Lisa Sheets

June 4–June 27, 1997
Opening Reception:
Friday, June 6, 5–7pm

PANTONE 116 C
PANTONE 3005 C

AD, D, P: Heather Heflin DF: Cornish College of the Arts, Publications Dept. CL: Cornish College of the Arts   USA 1997

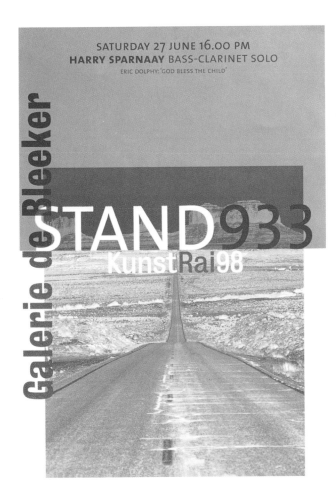

SATURDAY 27 JUNE 16.00 PM
HARRY SPARNAAY BASS-CLARINET SOLO
ERIC DOLPHY: 'GOD BLESS THE CHILD'

Galerie de Bleeker

STAND933
KunstRai98

KUNSTRAI JUNE 98

ALEX ARCADIA NYC
GUSTAVE ASSELBERGS
HERBERT NOUWENS

Alex Arcadia NYC / Gustave
Asselbergs / Jan Cremer
Hugo Kaagman / Mark Kolthoff
Charlotte van Pallandt
Lucebert / Herbert Nouwens
Nono Reinhold / Jan Sierhuis
OCEANIC ART

GALERIE DE BLEEKER HEEMSTEDE
Bleekersvaartweg 18, 2101 c9 Heemstede the Netherlands
Donderdag t/m zondag 12-5 uur, (023) 528 59 80 *Willem Snitker*

VLM Computer Graphics
Nieuwe Herengracht 47
1011 RN Amsterdam

T (020) 427 22 90
F (020) 427 22 92
E info@vlm.nl

vLm

Jelle Post
Koen Vroeijenstijn
Candide Rietdijk

book mark

http://www.vlm.nl

1. CD, AD, D: Michaël Snitker DF: Snitker Graphic Design CL: Kunstrai / Galerie de Bleeker   Netherlands 1998

PANTONE Process Magenta C
PANTONE 8280 C

2. CD, AD, D: Michaël Snitker DF: Snitker Graphic Design CL: VLM   Netherlands 1998

PANTONE Process Black C
PANTONE 8241 C

PANTONE 192 C
PANTONE Process Black C

1. AD, D, P: Heather Heflin P: Kurt Smith CW: Jane Buckman DF: Cornish College of the Arts Publications Dept. CL: Cornish College of the Arts USA 1997

PANTONE 181 C
PANTONE 142 C

2. D: Andreas Trogisch / Jan Warner DF: Grappa Blotto CL: Geor Kallweit Germany 1998

1. CD, AD, D: Michaël Snitker DF: Snitker Graphic Design CL: Galerie de Bleeker   Netherlands 1997

PANTONE 809 C
PANTONE 8001 C

2. 3. AD, D, P: Tirso Francés / Robin Uleman AD: Ron Faas DF: Dietwee CL: Winkel van Sinkel   Netherlands 1998

PANTONE Process Black C
PANTONE Process Blue C

PANTONE Process Black C
PANTONE 380 C

PANTONE Process Black C
PANTONE 630 C

1. CD: Sachiko Mikami   AD: Nobuo Seto   DF: Twinkle   CL: Culture Publishers   Japan 1997

PANTONE Orange 021 C
PANTONE 8361 C

2. D: Shoji Tsumura   CL: R · C · S   Japan 1997

1. 2. AD, D, I: Ichiro Watanabe I, CW: Makoto Hirata DF: Ichiro Watanabe Graphics CL: M&R Co. , Ltd.
Japan 1996 (1) 1998 (2)

PANTONE 2746 U
PANTONE 115 U
PANTONE 2727 U
PANTONE 3405 U

3. CD: Shuntaro Kanai AD, D: Naohiro Ukawa CL: Albatros Film Japan 1998

PANTONE Process Black U
PANTONE Process Magenta U

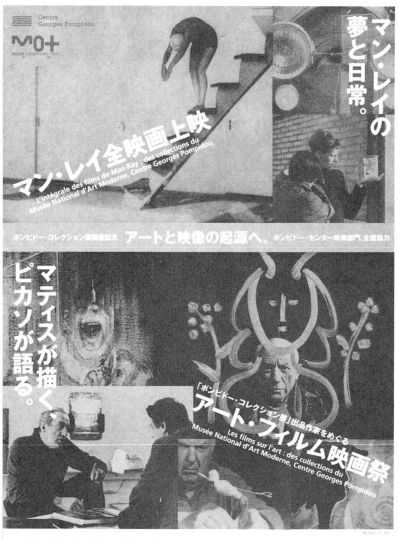

 PANTONE Process Black U / PANTONE 877 C
 PANTONE Process Black U / PANTONE 8361 C
 PANTONE Process Black U / PANTONE 8220 C
 PANTONE Process Black U / PANTONE 8081 C

CD, CW: Futoshi Koga AD, D: Masayuki Uchida DF: Voltage Co., Ltd. CL: Asahi Shimbun   Japan 1997

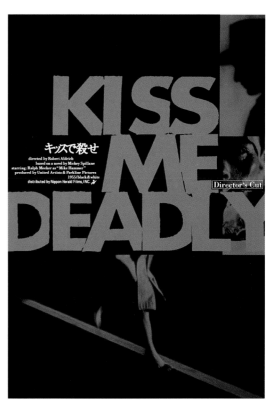

1. AD, D: Kyoko Iida DF: Atelier Kd Ltd. CL: Ilia Flamencos Club   Japan 1998

PANTONE 2985 U
PANTONE Process Black U

2. AD: Eiji Sakagawa CL: Nippon Herald Films. Inc.   Japan 1998

PANTONE 306 C
PANTONE Process Black C

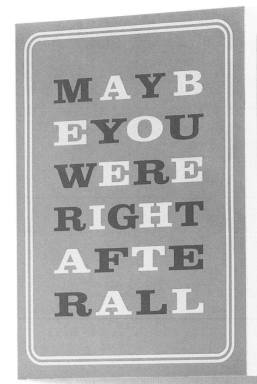

PANTONE 628 U
PANTONE 166 U

CL, DF: Planet Design Co.   USA 1997

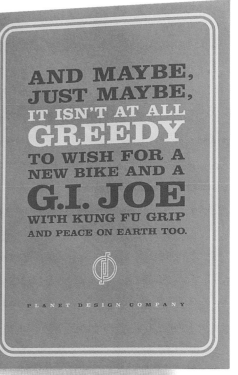

AND MAYBE
WIPING YOUR NOSE
ON YOUR GLOVE
IS SOMETIMES GOOD ENOUGH
AND MAYBE THE
GROWN-UP
TABLE
ISN'T ALL IT'S
CRACKED UP TO BE
AND MAYBE THAT
FANCY SCOOP OF
BUTTER
REALLY IS ICE CREAM.

AND MAYBE
SPITTING
OUT THE CHOCOLATES
YOU DON'T LIKE
MAKES PERFECT SENSE
AND MAYBE
TREES
REALLY DO CRY WHEN THEY
GET CUT DOWN
AND MAYBE
BATMAN
SMELLS AFTER ALL.

AND MAYBE,
JUST MAYBE,
IT ISN'T AT ALL
GREEDY
TO WISH FOR A
NEW BIKE AND A
G.I. JOE
WITH KUNG FU GRIP
AND PEACE ON EARTH TOO.

PLANET DESIGN COMPANY

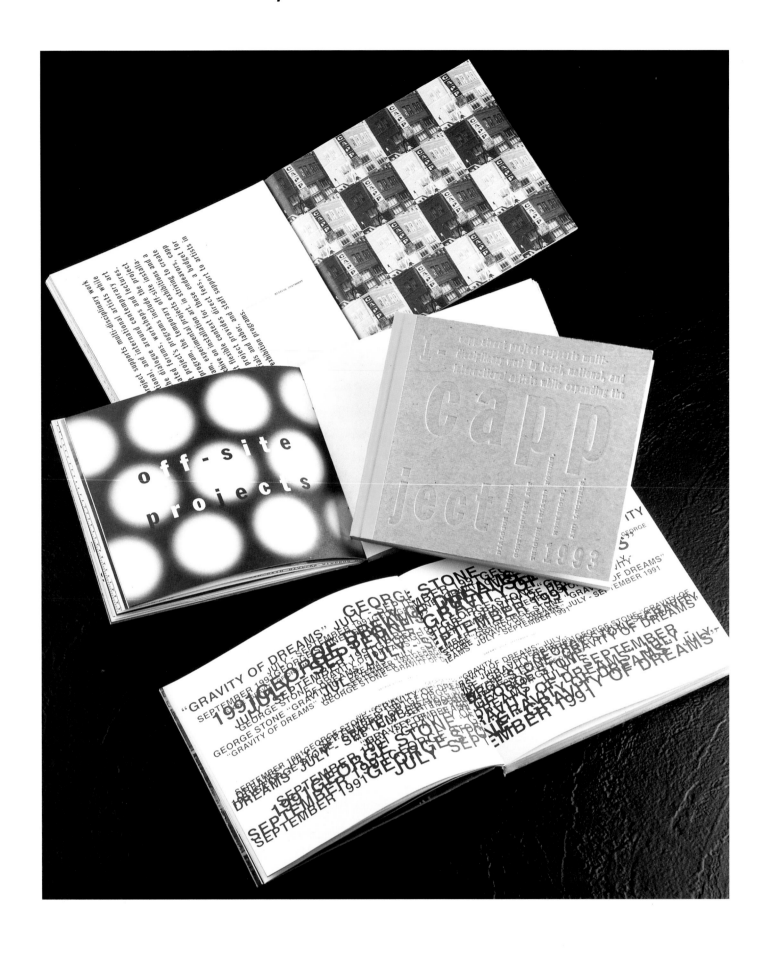

PANTONE Process Black C | AD, D: Jennifer Morla D: Craig Bailey CW: Constance Lewallen DF: Morla Design CL: Capp Street Project   USA 1995

1. CD, AD, D: John Ball D: Kathy Carpentier - Moore CW: Brian Woolsey DF: Mires Design, Inc. CL: First World USA 1997

PANTONE Process Black C
PANTONE 877 C

2. CD, AD, D: Hoi L. Chu I: James H. Keeton DF: HLC Group Inc. CL: Whatman Inc. USA 1996

PANTONE 299 U
PANTONE Cool Gray 11 U

3. CD, AD, D: R. Verkaart DF: Stoere Binken Design CL: Newman College Netherlands 1997

PANTONE 130 C
PANTONE 295 C

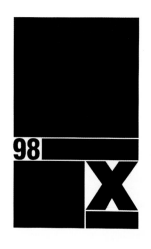

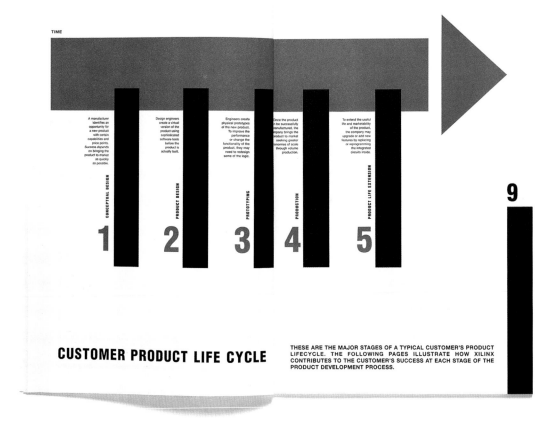

A manufacturer identifies an opportunity for a new product with certain capabilities and price points. Success depends on bringing the product to market as quickly as possible.

CONCEPTUAL DESIGN

1

Design engineers create a virtual version of the new product using sophisticated software tools before the product is actually built.

PRODUCT DESIGN

2

Engineers create physical prototypes of the new product. To improve the performance or change the functionality of the product, they may need to redesign some of the logic.

PROTOTYPING

3

Once the product can be successfully manufactured, the company brings the product to market seeking greater economies of scale through volume production.

PRODUCTION

4

To extend the useful life and marketability of the product, the company may upgrade or add new features by replacing or reprogramming the integrated circuits inside.

PRODUCT LIFE EXTENSION

5

9

CUSTOMER PRODUCT LIFE CYCLE

THESE ARE THE MAJOR STAGES OF A TYPICAL CUSTOMER'S PRODUCT LIFECYCLE. THE FOLLOWING PAGES ILLUSTRATE HOW XILINX CONTRIBUTES TO THE CUSTOMER'S SUCCESS AT EACH STAGE OF THE PRODUCT DEVELOPMENT PROCESS.

5

PRODUCT FEATURES AND CAPABILITIES

19

BECAUSE XILINX KEEPS INCREASING THE SPEED AND DENSITY OF PROGRAMMABLE LOGIC DEVICES, XILINX CUSTOMERS CAN EXTEND THE LIFE OF THEIR PRODUCTS AND EARN A HIGHER RETURN ON THEIR DEVELOPMENT INVESTMENT BY REPLACING THE ORIGINAL DEVICES WITH FASTER, DENSER, AND LESS EXPENSIVE VERSIONS. CUSTOMERS REALIZE THE FULL VALUE OF WORKING WITH XILINX, AND PLAN FUTURE PRODUCTS USING XILINX DEVICES, SOFTWARE, AND SUPPORT.

PANTONE 1665 U
PANTONE Process Black U

AD: Bill Cahan D: Michael Braley CW: Thom Elkjer DF: Cahan & Associates CL: Xilinx   USA 1998

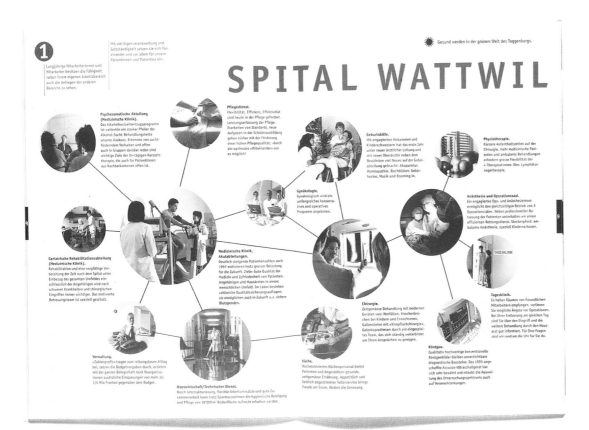

Gesund werden in der grünen Welt des Toggenburgs.

SPITAL WATTWIL

Jahresbericht 1997

Spital-Versorgungsregion
Fürstenland-Toggenburg

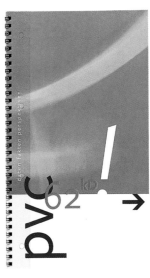

PVC-Verbrauch nach Branchen
Angaben in Prozent

	Deutschland	Schweiz	Österreich	Europa
Bauwesen	60	76	81	53
Transport, Auto	4	1	4	3
Verpackung	11	1	2	16
Elektro, Kabel	8	7	8	9
Möbel, Büro	3	4	2	3
Sonstiges	14	11	3	16

1. CD, AD, D: Lucia Frey / Heinz Wild P: Pascal Wüest DF: Wild & Frey, Agentur Für Design CL: Spital Flawil, Spital Wattwil, Spital Wil   Switzerland 1997

PANTONE Red 032 U
PANTONE 286 U

2. CD: Detlef Behr DF: Design Büro Behr CL: Arbeitsgemeinschaft Pvc + Umwelt   Germany 1996

PANTONE 158 U
PANTONE 280 U

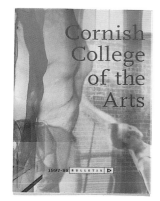

Cornish
College
of the
Arts

1997-98 BULLETIN ▷

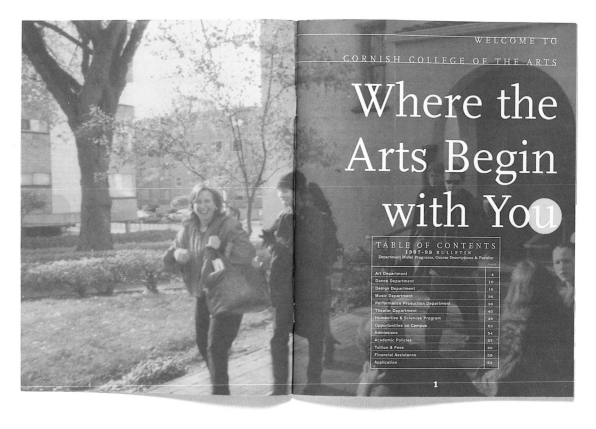

WELCOME TO
CORNISH COLLEGE OF THE ARTS

Where the Arts Begin with You

1

"WE ARE A COMMUNITY OF ARTISTS HERE AT CORNISH COLLEGE, WORKING AND CREATING TOGETHER...WE ARE ENRICHED BY THE DIALOGUE, DIVERSITY OF THOUGHTS AND VISIONS FOR THE FUTURE THAT THIS COMMUNITY HAS TO OFFER."

Sergei P. Tschernisch
President, Cornish College of the Arts

MISSION STATEMENT

THE MISSION OF CORNISH COLLEGE OF THE ARTS IS TO PROVIDE STUDENTS ASPIRING TO BECOME PRACTICING ARTISTS WITH AN EDUCATIONAL PROGRAM OF THE HIGHEST POSSIBLE QUALITY, IN AN ENVIRONMENT THAT NURTURES CREATIVITY AND INTELLECTUAL CURIOSITY, WHILE PREPARING THEM TO CONTRIBUTE TO SOCIETY AS ARTISTS, CITIZENS, AND INNOVATORS. CORNISH REALIZES THIS MISSION BY OFFERING BACCALAUREATE STUDIES IN THE PERFORMING AND VISUAL ARTS AND BY SERVING AS A FOCAL POINT IN THE COMMUNITY FOR PUBLIC PRESENTATION, ARTISTIC CRITICISM, PARTICIPATION, AND DISCUSSION OF THE ARTS.

2

JOIN US
IN CELEBRATION OF OUR PAST...

In 1914 Nellie Cornish, a woman of profound vision and unlimited energy, founded the "Cornish School of Music" in Seattle, Washington. Ballet and the visual arts were soon added to the curriculum, and in 1924 Cornish enrolled 1,000 students. The next three decades saw a parade of famous artists teaching or in residencies at the College, or students destined to be prestigious artists in attendance at the school: Pavlova, Martha Graham, John Cage, Merce Cunningham, Mark Tobey, Morris Graves, Thornton Wilder, Ben Hecht, Ruth St. Denis, Ted Shawn, Chet Huntley, and Imogen Cunningham, among others. In 1977 "Cornish Institute" was awarded full accreditation through the Northwest Association of Schools and Colleges. Since then Cornish College of the Arts has continued to build its reputation as a national focal point for arts education.

TAKE A LOOK
AT THE PRESENT...

Over 100 music concerts per year. A dozen theatrical performances. Fall and spring dance concerts. Hallways and galleries filled with student artwork. All in all, Cornish is a very exciting place to learn. Here is a special community of artists where the individuality and potential of each student as a whole person is realized and where personalized attention is provided. The College offers an education that is both flexible and rigorous, allowing individual vision to emerge from a solid grounding in technical skills while fostering the development of both critical thinking and the imagination.

UNITE WITH US
IN CREATING OUR FUTURE...

Cornish College is preparing to meet its goals for the 21st century by strengthening its partnership with students, faculty, staff, trustees, parents, and the greater community. Together we are moving Cornish to the next level of influence in the arts, both regionally and nationally. Cornish College will continue as a premier arts college, a place where students and faculty find the freedom, support, and challenge to create their art, a place to stretch artistically and intellectually, a place to find the resources necessary to meet the diverse educational and artistic needs of the 21st century.

3

AD, D, P: Heather Heflin D: Bonnie Dain P: C. Bennion / Spike Mafford / J, Maleri / K. Smith CW: Andy Gary / Lisa Pederson / Dana West
DF: Cornish College of the Arts, Publications Dept. CL: Cornish College of the Arts   USA 1997

PANTONE 395 U
PANTONE 5473 U

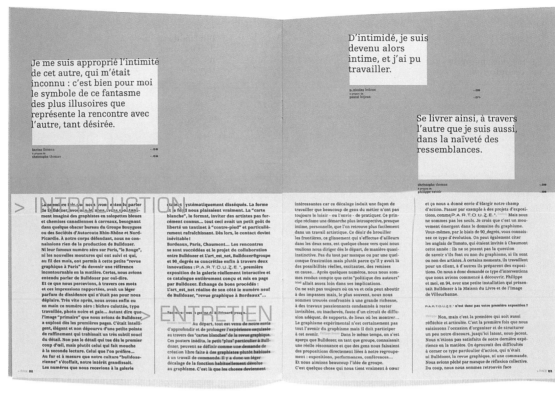

Je me suis approprié l'intimité de cet autre, qui m'était inconnu : c'est bien pour moi le symbole de ce fantasme des plus illusoires que représente la rencontre avec l'autre, tant désirée.

karine thénau
à propos de
christophe thomas

D'intimidé, je suis devenu alors intime, et j'ai pu travailler.

p. nicolas ledoux
à propos de
pascal bejean

Se livrer ainsi, à travers l'autre que je suis aussi, dans la naïveté des ressemblances.

christophe thomas
à propos de
philippe savoir

> INTRODUCTION

La première fois que vous m'en avez parlé de bulldozer, vous m'avez entendu parler de bulldozer, avec quelle spontanéité imaginé des graphistes en salopettes bleues et chemises canadiennes à carreaux, besognant dans quelque obscur bureau du Groupe Bouygues ou des Sociétés d'Autoroute Rhin-Rhône et Nord-Picardie. À notre corps défendant, nous ne connaissons rien de la production de Bulldozer. Ni leur fameux numéro zéro sur Paris, "le Rouge", ni les nouvelles moutures qui ont suivi et qui, au fil des mois, ont permis à cette petite "revue graphique à Paris" de devenir une référence incontournable en la matière. Certes, nous avions entendu parler de Bulldozer par ouï-dire. Très vite après, nous avons enfin eu en main ce numéro zéro : bichro culottée, typo travaillée, photo noire et gaie... Autant dire que l'image "primaire" que nous avions de Bulldozer a explosé dès les premières pages. C'était intelligent, élégant et non dépourvu d'une petite pointe de raffinement qui trahissait un très subtil souci du détail. Non pas le détail qui tue dès le premier coup d'œil, mais plutôt celui qui fait mouche à la seconde lecture. Celui que l'on préfère... Au fur et à mesure que notre culture "bulldoze-rienne" s'étoffait, notre intérêt grandissait. Les numéros que nous recevions à la galerie

et sont systématiquement disséqués. La forme et le fond nous plaisaient vraiment. La "carte blanche", le format, inviter des artistes pas forcément connus... tout ceci avait un petit goût de liberté un tantinet à "contre-pied" et particulièrement rafraîchissant. Dès lors, le contact devint inévitable !

> ENTRETIEN

Bordeaux, Paris, Chaumont... Les rencontres se sont succédées et le projet de collaboration entre Bulldozer et l'art_est_net, Bulldozer@groupe et 90_degrés se concrétise enfin à travers deux innovations : P.A.R.T.O.U.Z.E.", première exposition de la galerie réellement interactive et ce catalogue entièrement conçu et mis en page par Bulldozer. Échange des procédés : L'art_est_net réalise de son côté le numéro neuf de Bulldozer, "revue graphique à Bordeaux"...

Au départ, tout est venu de notre envie d'approfondir et de prolonger l'expérience esquissée au travers des "cartes blanches" de la revue graphique. Ces posters inédits, le petit "plus" particulier à Bulldozer, peuvent se définir comme une demande de création libre faite à des graphistes plutôt habitués à un travail de commande. Il y a donc un léger décalage de la fonction habituellement dévolue au graphisme. C'est là que les choses deviennent

intéressantes car ce décalage induit une façon de travailler que beaucoup de gens du métier n'ont pas toujours le loisir - ou l'envie - de pratiquer. Ce principe réclame une démarche plus introspective, presque intime, personnelle, que l'on retrouve plus facilement dans un travail artistique. Ce désir de brouiller les frontières, ce glissement qui s'effectue d'ailleurs dans les deux sens, est quelque chose vers quoi nous voulions nous diriger dès le départ, de manière quasi-instinctive. Pas du tout par manque ou par une quelconque frustration mais plutôt parce qu'il y avait là des possibilités réelles, excitantes, des remises en cause... Après quelques numéros, nous nous sommes rendus compte que cette "politique des auteurs" allait assez loin dans ses implications. On ne sait pas toujours où on va et cela peut aboutir à des impasses mais, le plus souvent, nous nous sommes trouvés confrontés à une grande richesse, à des travaux passionnants condamnés à rester invisibles, ou inachevés, faute d'un circuit de diffusion adéquat, de supports, de lieux où les montrer... Le graphisme expérimental n'est certainement pas tout l'avenir du graphisme mais il doit participer à cet avenir. Dans le même temps, on s'est aperçu que Bulldozer, en tant que groupe, connaissait une réelle résonance et que des gens nous faisaient des propositions directement liées à notre regroupement : expositions, performances, conférences... Et nous aimions beaucoup l'idée de groupe. C'est quelque chose qui nous tient vraiment à cœur

et ça nous a donné envie d'élargir notre champ d'action. Passer par exemple à des projets d'expositions, comme P.A.R.T.O.U.Z.E." Mais nous ne sommes pas les seuls. Je crois que c'est un mouvement émergent dans le domaine du graphisme. Vous-mêmes, par le biais de 90_degrés, vous connaissez ce type d'évolution. On peut également citer les anglais de Tomato, qui étaient invités à Chaumont cette année : ils ne se posent pas la question de savoir s'ils font ou non du graphisme, si ils sont ou non des artistes. À certains moments, ils travaillent pour un client, à d'autres ils préparent des expositions. On nous a donc demandé ce type d'interventions que nous avions commencé à découvrir, Philippe et moi, en 94, avec une petite installation qui présentait Bulldozer à la Maison du Livre et de l'Image de Villeurbanne.

P.A.R.T.O.U.Z.E." n'est donc pas votre première exposition ?

Non, mais c'est la première qui soit aussi réfléchie et articulée. C'est la première fois que nous saisissons l'occasion d'organiser et de structurer un peu notre discours, jusqu'ici latent, sous-jacent. Nous n'étions pas satisfaits de notre dernière expérience en la matière. On éprouvait des difficultés à cerner ce type particulier d'action, qui n'était ni Bulldozer, la revue graphique, ni une commande. Nous avions péché par manque de réflexion collective. Du coup, nous nous sommes retrouvés face

PANTONE 397 U
PANTONE Process Black U

CD, AD, D, P, I: Misc. CW: 90° DF: Bulldozer CL: 90 degrés   France 1998

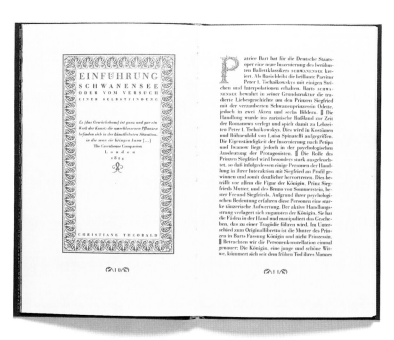

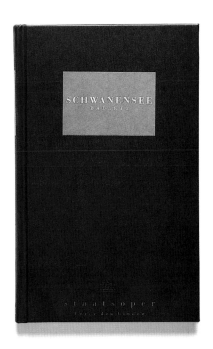

1. CD, AD, D, CW : Beatriz Gonzalez DF: Beatriz Gonzalez - Studio B CL: American Express Company   Mexico 1997

PANTONE Process Black C
PANTONE 307 C

2. D, P, CW, DF: Cyan CL: State Opera Berlin   Germany 1997

PANTONE 2965 U
PANTONE 871 U

Jaarverslag 1994
BSO/ORIGIN ONDERNEMINGSRAAD

DE OR VOLGENS ZIJN VOORZITTER

Een multi-culturele ondernemingsraad, de eerste van BSO en Origin samen.
Een rijk geschakeerde groep, die royaal beantwoordt aan de verwachting dat een medezeggenschapper iets te zeggen heeft.

Vergadertechnisch niet altijd even gemakkelijk, maar boeiend, creatief en niet te "zwaarwichtig". Opererend in een open en constructieve verhouding met de bestuurder, waarbij de grenzen meer door de geest dan door de letter van de wet worden bepaald. Sommige OR-leden kijken naar de grote lijnen, anderen naar de details; vorm zowel als inhoud krijgen daarbij de vereiste aandacht. Dat verschillende culturen tot verschillende accenten leiden is natuurlijk en past uitstekend bij een voortgaande professionalisering. Maar hoe boeiend ook, de spanning tussen OR-werk en de eigen loopbaanontwikkeling blijft aanwezig en vraagt helaas zijn tol aan de zich daardoor niet herverkiesbaar stellenden.

DE OR VOLGENS DE BESTUURDER

Kritisch, lastig, meedenkend, nuttig.

Kritisch, omdat de ondernemingsraad niet met elk antwoord genoegen neemt, doorvraagt, details opvraagt om zich een beter oordeel te kunnen vormen.
Lastig, omdat, nadat er besluiten genomen zijn in het DO, het nodige voorbereid moet worden om een en ander bij de OR goed aan te leveren voor advies.
Meedenkend: de opmerkingen zijn altijd goed onderbouwd, waardoor de inbreng van de OR in het geheel genomen groter is dan menigeen denkt. Vooral in de diverse commissies wordt dat duidelijk.
Ondanks dat de OR kritisch is en lastig vanwege de extra hoeveelheid werk die hij genereert, maakt zijn meedenkende inzet dat de ondernemingsraad, zoals die bij BSO/Origin functioneert, als zeer nuttig wordt ervaren.

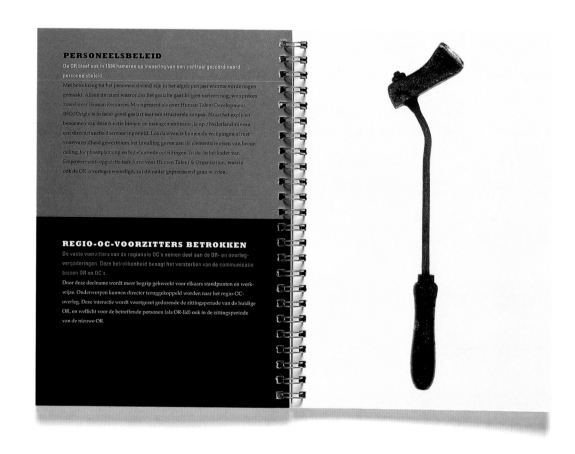

PERSONEELSBELEID

De OR bleef ook in 1994 hameren op invoering van een centraal gecoördineerd personeelsbeleid.

Met betrekking tot het personeelsbeleid zijn in het afgelopen jaar enorme vorderingen gemaakt. Alleen de naam waaronder het gestalte gaat krijgen varieert nog, we spreken zowel over Human Resources Management als over Human Talent Development. BSO/Origin is in ieder geval gestart met een structurele aanpak. Naast het expliciet benoemen van deze functie binnen de managementteams, is op /Nederland-niveau een directiefunctie daarvoor ingesteld. Los daarvan is binnen de vestigingen al met voortvarendheid gewerkt aan het invulling geven aan de elementaire eisen van beoordeling, loopbaanplanning en bijbehorende opleidingen. In de -in het kader van Empowerment- opgezette task force voor Human Talent & Organisation, waarin ook de OR is vertegenwoordigd, zal dit nader gepreciseerd gaan worden.

REGIO-OC-VOORZITTERS BETROKKEN

De vaste voorzitters van de regionale OC's nemen deel aan de OR- en overleg-vergaderingen. Deze betrokkenheid beoogt het versterken van de communicatie tussen OR en OC's.

Door deze deelname wordt meer begrip gekweekt voor elkaars standpunten en werkwijze. Onderwerpen kunnen directer teruggekoppeld worden naar het regio-OC-overleg. Deze interactie wordt voortgezet gedurende de zittingsperiode van de huidige OR, en wellicht voor de betreffende personen (als OR-lid) ook in de zittingsperiode van de nieuwe OR.

PANTONE Process Black U
PANTONE 4645 U

AD, D: Ron Faas / Tirso Francés / Richard van der Laken   P: Joost Meyer(Tools) / Sjaak Ramakers(Portrait)   CW: BSO / Origin Works Council
DF: Dietwee   CL: The Works Council of BSO / Origin   Netherlands 1995

OR-verkiezingen/37

OR-verkiezingen

Mede in het kader van de professionalisering van de medezeggenschap is continuiteit binnen de ondernemingsraad een vereiste, te bereiken met veel herverkiesbare kandidaten. Negen van de zeventien zittende leden gaven gehoor aan deze wens en werden allen herkozen. De overige kandidaten waren overigens ook van goed medezeggenschapskaliber, te weten drie leden uit vorige OR'en, drie recentelijke OC-leden. Drie enthousiaste (vrouwelijke) nieuwelingen als aanwinst maakten de club compleet.

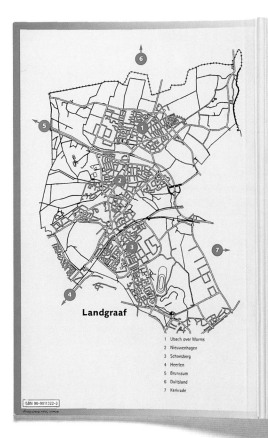

Landgraaf

1 Ubach over Worms
2 Nieuwenhagen
3 Schaesberg
4 Heerlen
5 Brunssum
6 Duitsland
7 Kerkrade

ISBN 90-9011322-3

1. AD, D: Ron Faas / Tirso Francés / Katja Berest P: Divers CW: BSO / Origin Works Council DF: Dietwee
CL: The Works Council of BSO / Origin   Netherlands 1997

PANTONE Process Black U
PANTONE 3288 U

PANTONE Process Black U
PANTONE 5415 U

2. CD, AD, D: R.Verkaart DF: Stoere Binken Design CL: Newman College   Netherlands 1997

PANTONE Process Black C
PANTONE 369 C

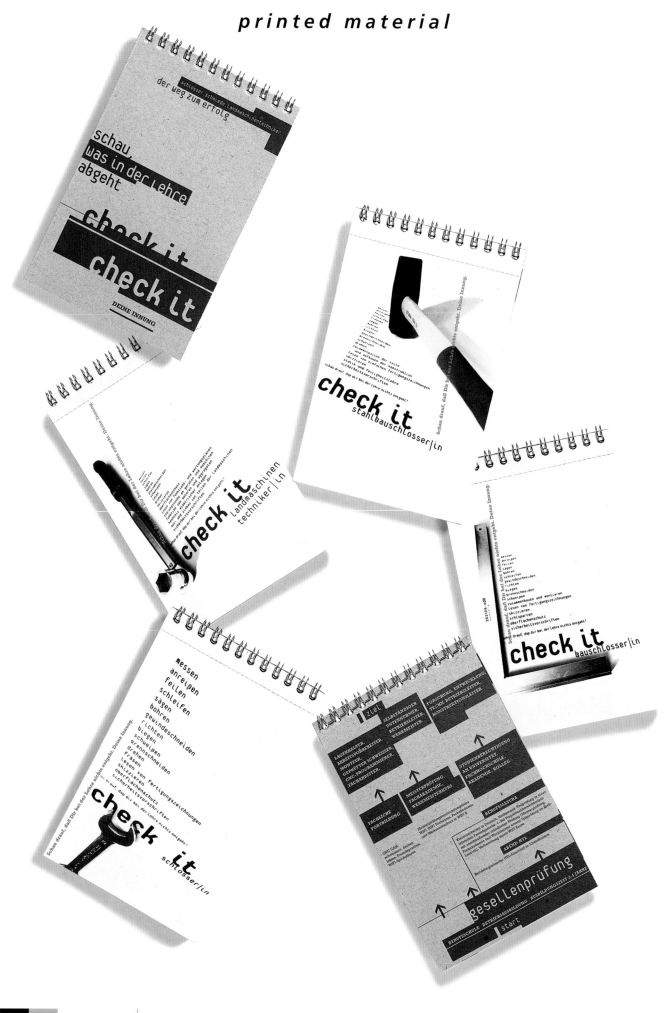

PANTONE Process Black U
PANTONE 151 U

AD, D : Sigi Ramoser / Klaus Österle P: Marc Lins CW: Hermann Brändle DF: Atelier Für Text Uno Gestaltung CL: Schlosserinnung   Austria 1998

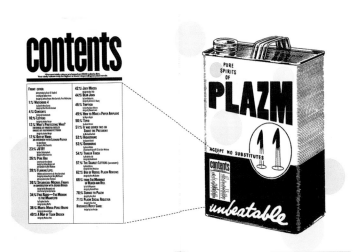

contents

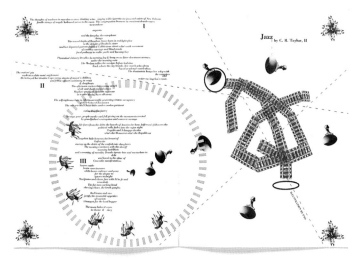

AD: Joshua Berger / Niko Courtelis D, I: Richard Kidd (1) / Imin Pao (3) D:Smokebomb (2)
DF: Plazm CL: Plazm Magazine   USA 1995 (1.3) 96 (2)

PANTONE Process Black C   PANTONE Process Black C   PANTONE Process Black C
                                                                  PANTONE 485 C

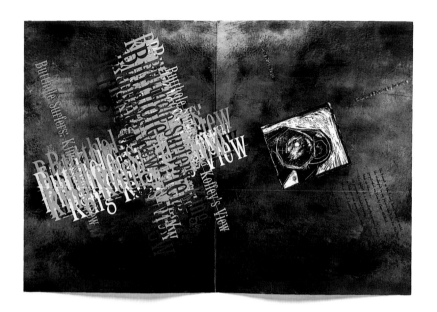

PANTONE Process Black C
PANTONE 485 C

1. CD, AD: Eugene Wang D, I: Robynne Raye P: Glenn James / NBA Photos CW: Jonathan Eig DF: Modern Dog
CL: "Unlimited" Magazine   USA 1997

PANTONE Process Black C
PANTONE 116 C

2. AD, D: Joshua Berger I: Joe Sorren DF: Plazm CL: Plazm Magazine   USA 1994

PANTONE Process Black C
PANTONE 116 C

3. AD, P: Joshua Berger AD: Niko Courtelis D: John Boiler DF: Plazm CL: Plazm Magazine   USA 1994

CD, D, P, CW: Misc. AD: Bulldozer CL: Signes   France 1997

PANTONE 1375 C
PANTONE 2695 C

PANTONE 122 C
PANTONE 2766 C

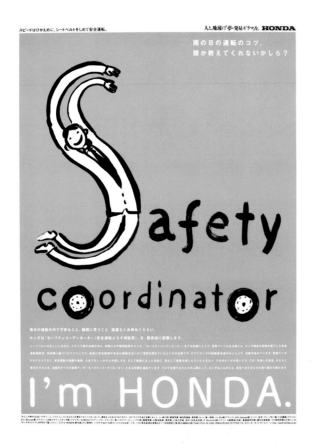

PANTONE Process Black U	PANTONE Process Black U	PANTONE Process Black U	PANTONE Process Black U
PANTONE Process Blue U	PANTONE 2915 U	PANTONE Process Cyan U	PANTONE 306 U
PANTONE Process Black U	PANTONE Process Black U	PANTONE Process Black U	PANTONE Process Black U
PANTONE 211 U	PANTONE 306 U	PANTONE Warm Red U	PANTONE Red 032 U

CD: Minoru Fujii / Koji Takahashi AD, I: Kazunari Hattori D: Reijiro Oba CW: Yasuhito Isobe / Ako Okada DF: Light Publicity Ltd. Japan 1996-97

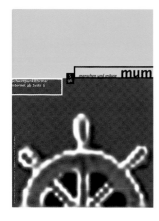

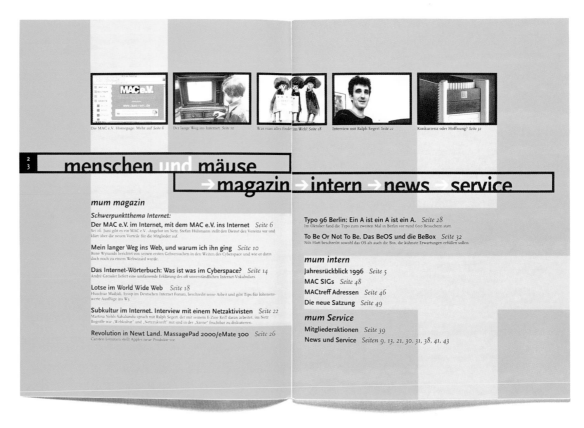

Die MAC e.V. Homepage. Mehr auf *Seite 6* — Der lange Weg ins Internet. *Seite 10* — Was man alles findet im Web! *Seite 18* — Interview mit Ralph Segert *Seite 22* — Konkurrenz oder Hoffnung? *Seite 32*

menschen und mäuse
→ magazin → intern → news → service

mum magazin

Schwerpunktthema Internet:

Der MAC e.V. im Internet, mit dem MAC e.V. ins Internet *Seite 6*
Seit 16. Juni gibt es ein MAC e.V. -Angebot im Netz. Stefan Hülsmann stellt den Dienst des Vereins vor und klärt über die neuen Vorteile für die Mitglieder auf.

Mein langer Weg ins Web, und warum ich ihn ging *Seite 10*
René Wynands berichtet von seinen ersten Gehversuchen in den Weiten des Cyberspace und wie er dann doch noch zu einem Webwizard wurde.

Das Internet-Wörterbuch: Was ist was im Cyberspace? *Seite 14*
André Gressler liefert eine umfassende Erklärung des oft unverständlichen Internet-Vokabulars.

Lotse im World Wide Web *Seite 18*
Huschiar Madjidi, Sysop im Deutschen Internet Forum, beschreibt seine Arbeit und gibt Tips für lohnenswerte Ausflüge ins W3.

Subkultur im Internet. Interview mit einem Netzaktivisten *Seite 22*
Martina Nehls-Sahaloandu sprach mit Ralph Segert, der mit seinem E-Zine KriT daran arbeitet, im Netz Begriffe wie „Webkultur" und „Netzzukunft" mit und in der „Szene" fruchtbar zu diskutieren.

Revolution in Newt Land. MassagePad 2000/eMate 300 *Seite 26*
Carsten Lemmen stellt Apple's neue Produkte vor.

Typo 96 Berlin: Ein A ist ein A ist ein A. *Seite 28*
Im Oktober fand die Typo zum zweiten Mal in Berlin vor rund 600 Besuchern statt.

To Be Or Not To Be. Das BeOS und die BeBox *Seite 32*
Nils Hott beschreibt sowohl das OS als auch die Box, die kühnste Erwartungen erfüllen sollen.

mum intern

Jahresrückblick 1996 *Seite 5*
MAC SIGs *Seite 48*
MACtreff Adressen *Seite 46*
Die neue Satzung *Seite 49*

mum Service

Mitgliederaktionen *Seite 39*
News und Service *Seiten 9, 13, 21, 30, 31, 38, 41, 43*

Typo 96 Berlin:
Ein A ist ein A ist ein A.

TYPO Berlin 96

PANTONE Process Black C
PANTONE 123 C

CD, AD, D, I, CW: Silke Löhmann / René Wynando's DF: Oktober - Kommunikations Design CL: MAC e. v.   Germany 1997

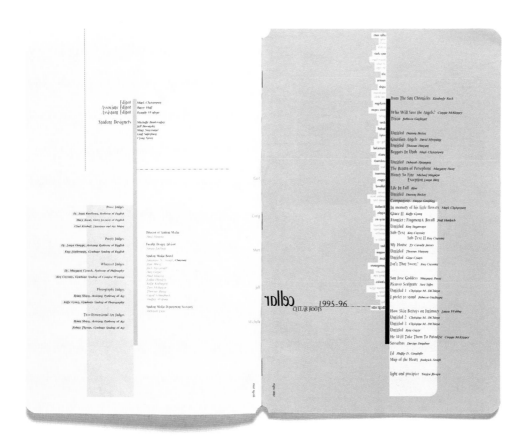

CD: Sue La Porte D: Gail Salenbien / Michelle Ritch / Jeff Bossardet / Matt Normand / Craig Steen DF: Student Project
CL: Eastern Michigan University   USA 1996

PANTONE Black 5 U
PANTONE 353 U

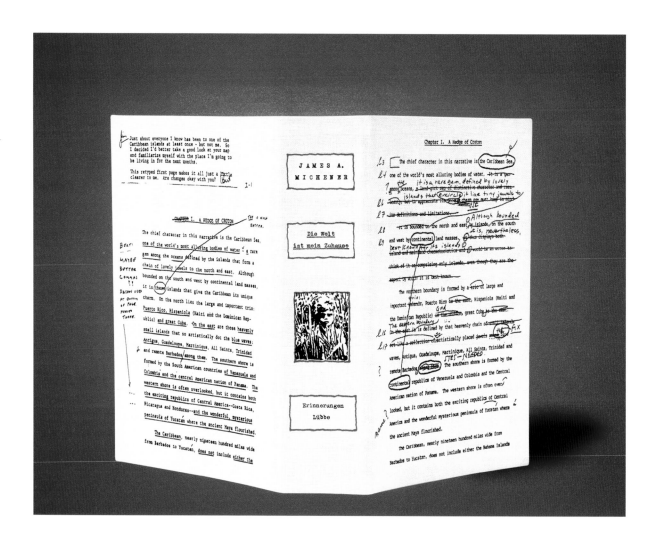

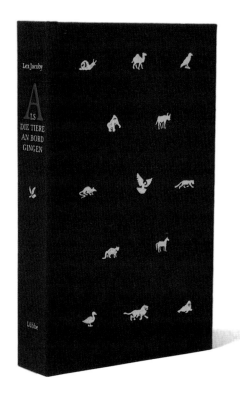

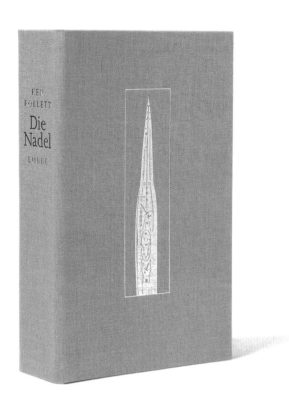

PANTONE Black 2 C	PANTONE 123 C	PANTONE 877 C
PANTONE 179 C	PANTONE 186 C	PANTONE 186 C

D, I: Achim Frederic Kiel DF: Pencil Corporate Art CL: Gustav Luebbe Verlag   Germany 1995

CD,AD, D, P,CW: Jue Becker / Pascal Béjean CL: Bulldozer®éditions   France 1997

PANTONE 176 U		PANTONE 319 U	
PANTONE 289 U		PANTONE Process Black U	

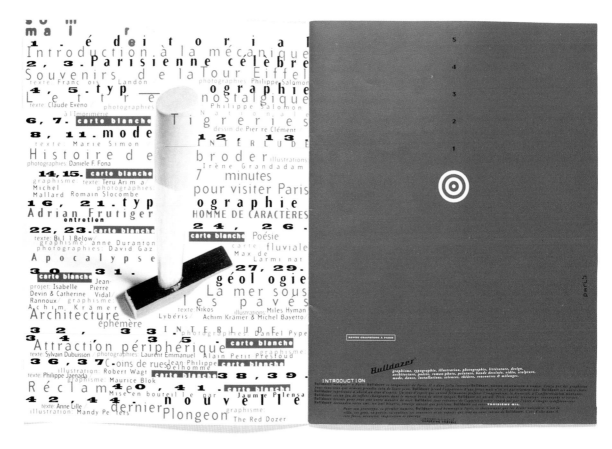

PANTONE Red 032 C

PANTONE Process Black C

CD, D, P, I, CW: Misc. CD: Frédéric Bortolotti CL: Bulldozer®éditions   France 1995 - 98

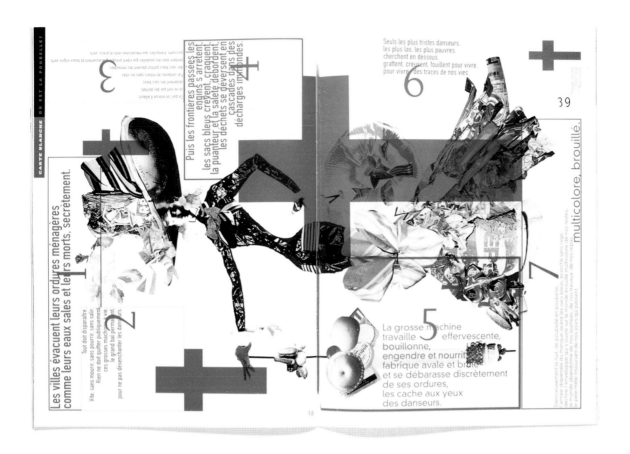

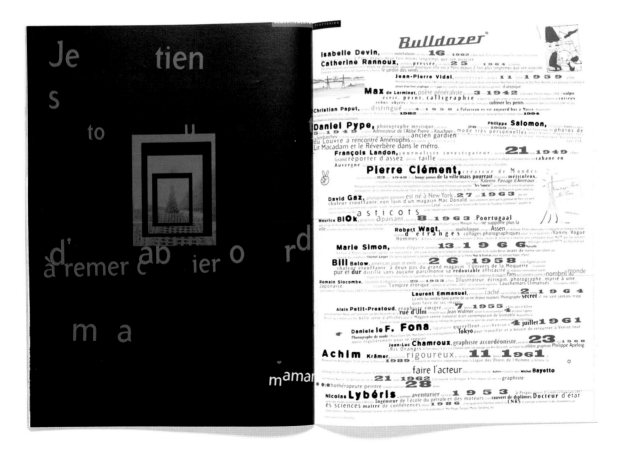

PANTONE 877 C
PANTONE 872 C

CD, AD, D: Ilja Sallacz CW, DF: Artur CL: Artur - Forum Für Kunst + Kultur   Germany 1997

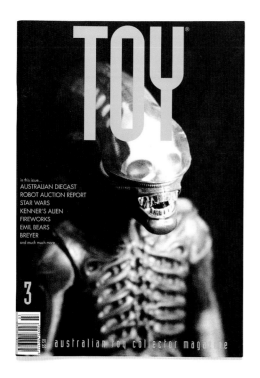

CD, AD, D: Joseph Colaric P: John Scarpa DF: Atomic Toy Design CL: Toy Magazine   Australia 1997

AD: Troy Bailly D: Stephen Parkes D, I: David Papineau P: Shane Jackson (1.2) / Barry Gnyp (2) DF: Prototype Design
CL: Capsule Magazine   Canada 1998

PANTONE 1945 C
PANTONE 2768 C
PANTONE 399 C
PANTONE 281 C

Jimi Hendrix's signature felt hat typifys the 17,000 pieces in the EMP permanent collection.

A letter from EMP Executive Director, Jo Allen Patton.

Hi, and welcome to a special collections issue of *Feedback*. This time around we want to show you what goes into building a world-class, multidisciplinarian music museum from the ground up. As EMP's executive director, part of my job — and that of our curators — involves going to auctions and executing calculated bids in order to fill EMP's Collections exhibitions with thousands of rare and popular music artifacts. The great part of working here for all of us — on a project that started three years ago — has been setting out to create something unprecedented. In this issue, we look at the hard work (and luck) that goes into collecting instruments played by revolutionary musicians as well as hunting down rare recordings, posters, documentary film footage, resource materials (volumes of music publications and fanzines), manuscripts, and various personal materials from musicians whose impact has been felt locally and globally.

Pete Blecha, curator of collections, tells us about a day in a curator's life and how he goes about bringing the museum some of its most prized showpieces. In Quartertime, you'll get an insider's view of how, exactly, we sat down in the beginning and came up with what we wanted to have in our museum, how we planned to categorize the pieces, and which criteria we use to determine if an item is a worthy collectible and not simply another rock 'n' roll curiosity. Then

there's the follow-through — what happens to an artifact after it comes through our front doors.

All of us working to build the Experience Music Project have high expectations for this museum. As we continue our search for all forms of pop-culture artifacts, we're thrilled that so many of you who have heard about us have contacted us with tips about what's out there or offerings from your own collections. All of us here at EMP have worked hard at raising public awareness about what we're doing — because we rely on your support in gathering a museum filled with collectibles that will, in a few years' time, rock this world.

— Jody

EMP staffers loiter impatiently in the lobby of the Rock & Roll Hall of Fame, awaiting their private tour of the exhibits.

Staff and consultants analyze plans, budgets and sketches during the three-day session.

Chief curator Jim Fricke entertains the team during the brainstorm.

eMp

Photos by Max Cameron.

Scopes Out the Rock and Roll Hall of Fame

In September, EMP staffers traveled to Cleveland, Ohio, to check out the newly opened Rock and Roll Hall of Fame and Museum, peruse their collections and meet their team. EMP curators, managers and consultants then sequestered themselves along the shore of Lake Erie for an intense week of exhibit brainstorming and planning.

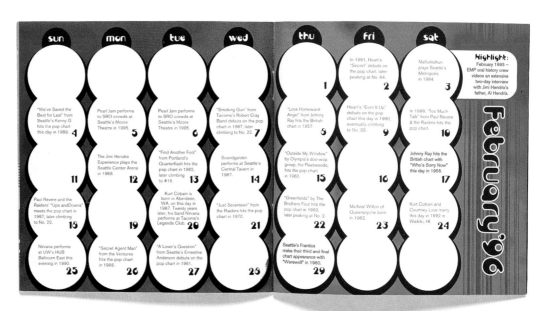

sun	mon	tue	wed	thu	fri	sat
				1 In 1991, Heart's "Secret" debuts on the pop chart, later peaking at No. 64.	**2**	**3** Malfunkshun plays Seattle's Metropolis in 1984.
4 "We've Saved the Best for Last" from Seattle's Kenny G hits the pop chart this day in 1989.	**5** Pearl Jam performs to SRO crowds at Seattle's Moore Theatre in 1995.	**6** Pearl Jam performs to SRO crowds at Seattle's Moore Theatre in 1995.	**7** "Smoking Gun" from Tacoma's Robert Cray Band debuts on the pop chart in 1987, later climbing to No. 22.	**8** "Look Homeward Angel" from Johnny Ray hits the British chart in 1957.	**9** Heart's "Even It Up" debuts on the pop chart this day in 1980, eventually climbing to No. 33.	**10** In 1968, "Too Much Talk" from Paul Revere & the Raiders hits the pop chart.
11	**12** The Jimi Hendrix Experience plays the Seattle Center Arena in 1968.	**13** "Find Another Fool" from Portland's Quarterflash hits the pop chart in 1982, later climbing to #16.	**14** Soundgarden performs at Seattle's Central Tavern in 1987.	**15** "Outside My Window" by Olympia's doo-wop group, the Fleetwoods, hits the pop chart in 1960.	**16**	**17** Johnny Ray hits the British chart with "Who's Sorry Now" this day in 1958.
18 Paul Revere and the Raiders' "Ups andDowns" meets the pop chart in 1967, later climbing to No. 22.	**19**	**20** Kurt Cobain is born in Aberdeen, WA, on this day in 1967. Twenty years later, his band Nirvana performs at Tacoma's Legends Club.	**21** "Just Seventeen" from the Raiders hits the pop chart in 1970.	**22** "Greenfields" by The Brothers Four hits the pop chart in 1960, later peaking at No. 2.	**23** Micheal Wilton of Queensryche born in 1962.	**24** Kurt Cobain and Courtney Love marry this day in 1992 in Waikiki, HI.
25 Nirvana performs at UW's HUB Ballroom East this evening in 1990.	**26** "Secret Agent Man" from the Ventures hits the pop chart in 1966.	**27** "A Lover's Question" from Seattle's Ernestine Anderson debuts on the pop chart in 1981.	**28**	**29** Seattle's Frantics make their third and final chart appearance with "Werewolf" in 1960.		

Highlight: February 1993 — EMP oral history crew videos an extensive two-day interview with Jimi Hendrix's father, Al Hendrix.

February '96

PANTONE 355 C
PANTONE 1795 C

CD, CW: Emp AD, DF: Modern Dog D, I: Michael Strassburger / Robynne Raye / Vittorio Costarella / George Estrada CL: Experience Music Project USA 1995

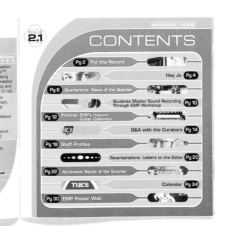

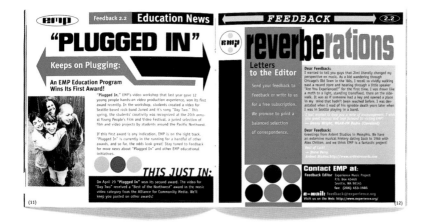

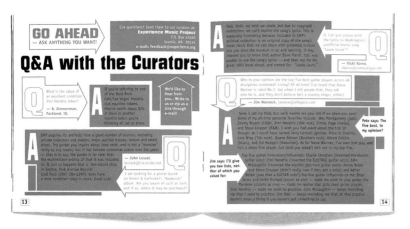

CD, CW: Emp AD, DF: Modern Dog D, I: Michael Strassburger / Robynne Raye / Vittorio Costarella / George Estrada / Coby Schultz (1) CL: Experience Music Project USA 1996

PANTONE 102 C		PANTONE 299 C	
PANTONE Process Black C		PANTONE Process Black C	

PANTONE Process Black U
PANTONE 877 U

PANTONE Process Black U
PANTONE Blue 072 U

PANTONE Process Black U
PANTONE 877 U

PANTONE 355 U
PANTONE 172 U

E

PANTONE Blue 072 U
PANTONE 107 U

E

PANTONE Process Black U
PANTONE 279 U

CD, AD, D, I: Wout de Vringer DF: Faydherbe / De Vringer CL: Stadscollectie Den Haag   Netherlands 1997

AD, D : Sigi Ramoser / Klaus Österle DF: Atelier Für Text und Gestaltung CL: Messerle GmbH
Austria 1998

PANTONE 330 C | 1. CD: Patricia Belyea D, I: Christian Salas DF: Belyea Design Alliance CL: Maison de France   USA 1998

PANTONE 660 U
PANTONE Process Black U | 2. CD, AD, D, I: Andrea Villafane DF: Zero Design Studio CL: Alter Ego Video Productions   USA 1998

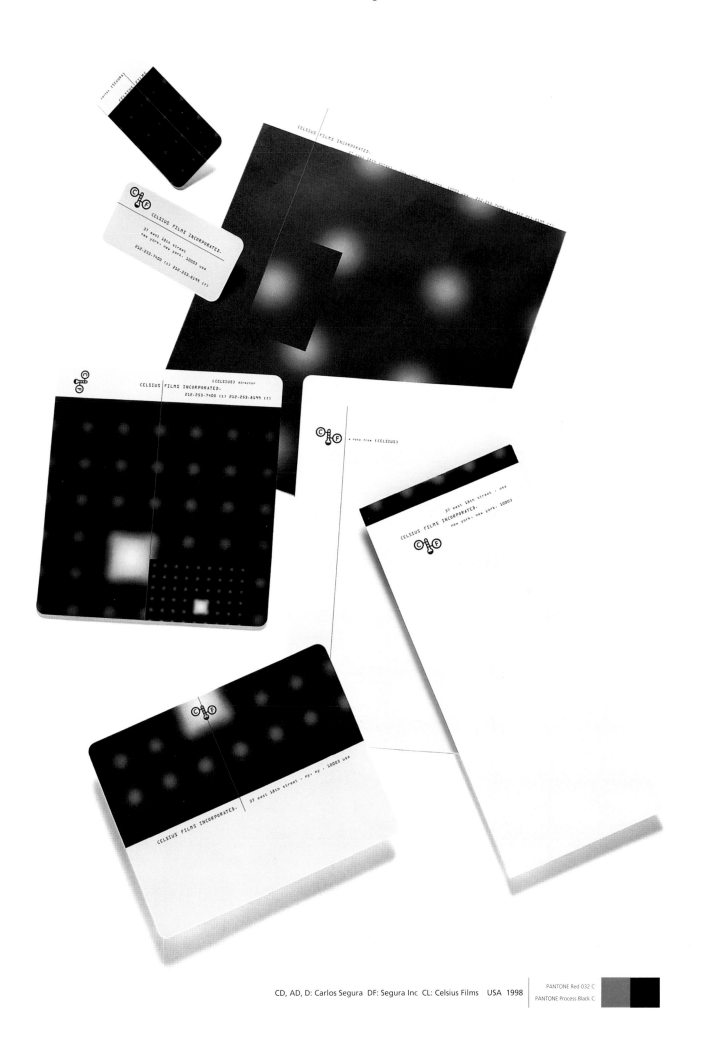

CD, AD, D: Carlos Segura DF: Segura Inc CL: Celsius Films   USA 1998

PANTONE Red 032 C
PANTONE Process Black C

PANTONE 5767 C
PANTONE Process Black C

CD: P. R. Brown CL: Bau - Da Design Lab,Inc . USA 1997

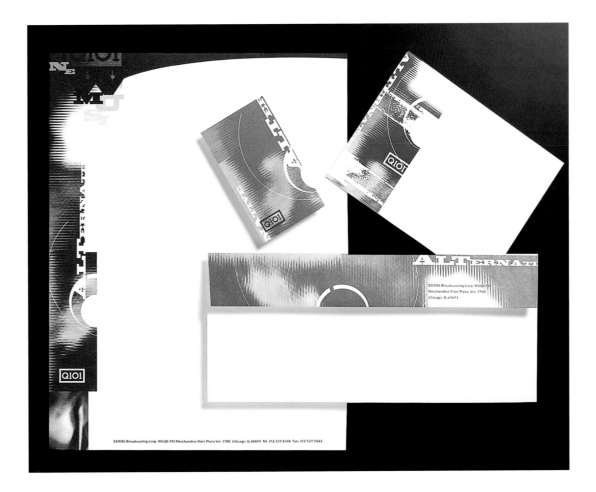

1. CD: Carlos Segura AD, D: Colin Metcalf DF: Segura Inc. CL: Q101   USA 1997

PANTONE 8200 C
PANTONE Process Black C

PANTONE 8101 C
PANTONE Process Black C

2. AD, D: Andrew Hoyne P: Marcus Sfruzina I: Dean Gorissen DF: Hoyne Design CL: Metropolis   Australia 1997

PANTONE 8483 C
PANTONE 8700 C

PANTONE Orange 021 U
PANTONE Process Black U

CD: Carlos Segura AD, D: Colin Metcalf DF: Segura Inc. CL: Spontaneous Combustion   USA 1997

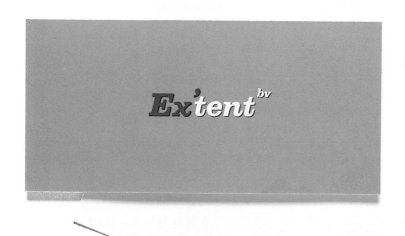

1. CD, AD, D: Kristina Teubner / Katrin Wiens DF: Tour - Salon CL: Das Computerspiele Museum   Germany 1998

PANTONE 2925 C
PANTONE Process Black C

2. AD, D: Ron Faas / Harmen Liemburg AD: Tirso Francés DF: Dietwee CL: Ex'tent   Netherlands 1997

PANTONE 311 U
PANTONE 463 U

PANTONE Process Black U
PANTONE 151 U

1. CD, AD, D, I: John Sayles DF: Sayles Graphic Design CL: Consolidated Correctional Food Service   USA 1997

PANTONE Process Black U
PANTONE 185 U

2. CD, AD, D, I: John Sayles DF: Sayles Graphic Design CL: Greater Des Moines Goodtime Jazz festival   USA 1997

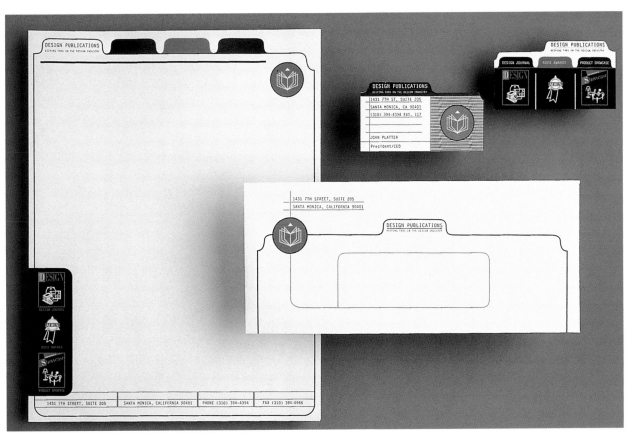

CD, AD, D, I: John Sayles DF: Sayles Graphic Design CL: Design Publications   USA 1997

PANTONE Process Black U

PANTONE 185 U

PANTONE 2905 U
PANTONE Orange 021 U

1. CD, AD, D: Wout De Vringer CD, I: Ton Hoogerwerf DF: Faydherbe / De Vringer CL: Ton of Holland   Netherlands 1998

PANTONE 310 U
PANTONE Orange 021 U

2. D: Katja Berest DF: Dietwee CL: The Dutch Photographers   Netherlands 1996

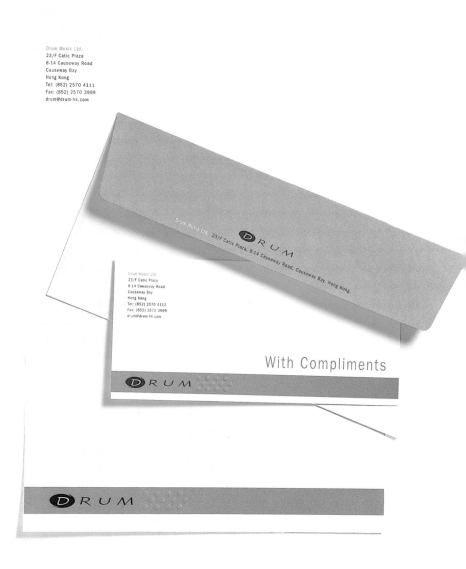

3. D: Kwok Chan CL: Drum Music Ltd.   Hong Kong 1997

PANTONE Orange 021 C

PANTONE Process Black C

PANTONE 876 C
PANTONE Process Black C

CD, AD, D: R. Verkaart DF: Stoere Binken Design CL: Net Facillities Group   Netherlands 1997

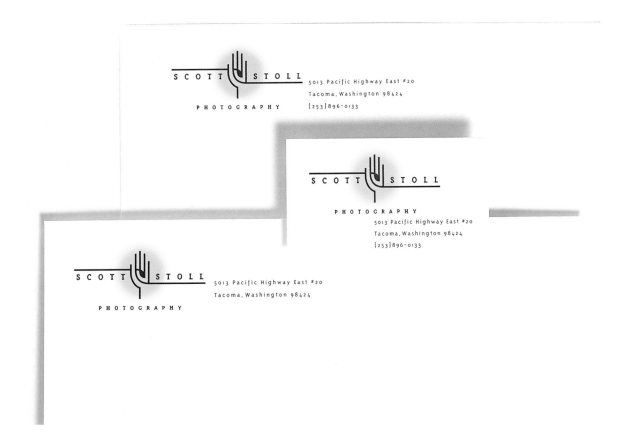

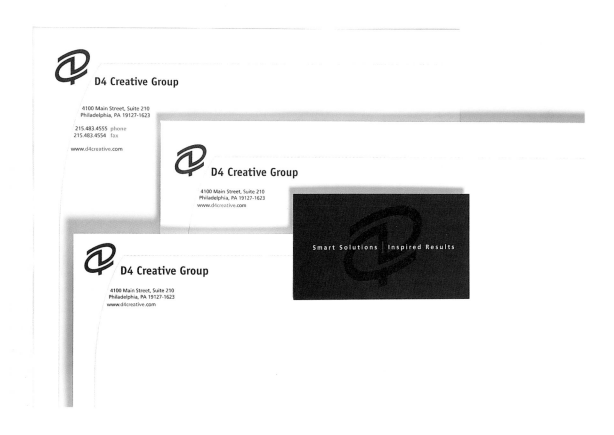

1. CD: Patricia Belyea D, I: Christian Salas DF: Belyea Design Alliance CL: Scott Stoll Photography   USA 1998

PANTONE Process Black U
PANTONE 113 U

2. AD, D, I: Wicky W. Lee CW: Paul Fitzgerald DF, CL: D4 Creative Group   USA 1998

PANTONE Process Black C
PANTONE 8400 C
*Virnish

PANTONE Process Black U | AD: Kevin Wade / Dana Lytle D: Martha Graettinger DF,CL: Planet Design Co.   USA 1997

1. DF: Planet Design Co. CL: Kaz Technologies   USA 1995

PANTONE Process Black U
PANTONE 471 U

2. DF: Planet Design Co. CL: Graphite Inc. Digital Solutions   USA 1996

PANTONE 457 U
PANTONE 8421 C

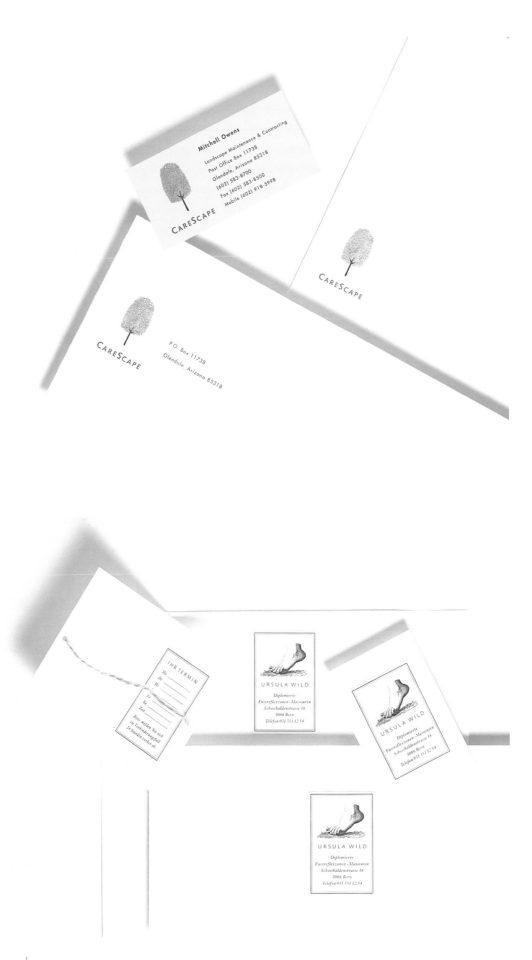

1. CD, AD: Forrest Richardson D, I: Nathan Naylor DF: Richardson or Richardson CL: Care Scape   USA 1997

2. CD, AD, D: Heinz Wild DF: Wild & Frey, Agentur Für Design CL: Ursula Wild   Switzerland 1996

PANTONE 385 U
PANTONE 4625 U

PANTONE 1797 U
PANTONE Process Black U

1. CD, AD, D, CW, CL: Trudy Cole - Zielanski DF: Trudy Cole - Zielanski Design   USA 1993 | PANTONE Process Black U

2. CD, AD, I: Catharine Bradbury D: Dean Bartsch DF: Bradbury Design Inc. CL: University of Regina Bookstore   Canada 1997 | PANTONE 3435 U

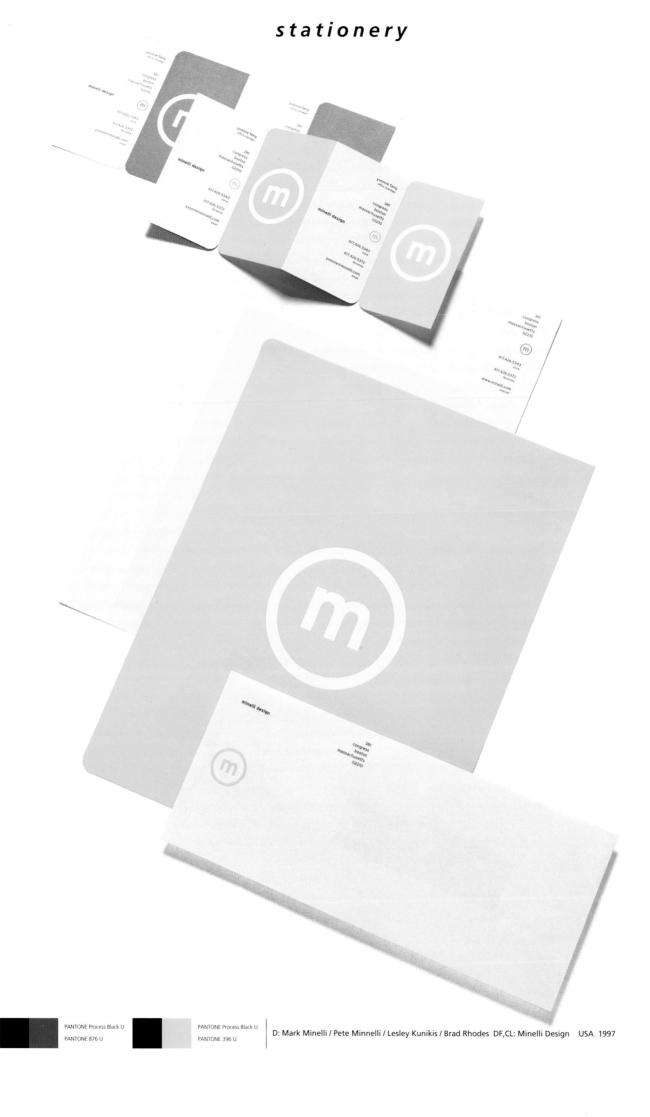

PANTONE Process Black U
PANTONE 876 U

PANTONE Process Black U
PANTONE 396 U

D: Mark Minelli / Pete Minnelli / Lesley Kunikis / Brad Rhodes DF,CL: Minelli Design   USA 1997

1. D: Tilman Wendland / Andreas Trogisch / Heike Grebin
DF, CL: Grappa Blotto   Germany 1998

PANTONE 3242 C
PANTONE Process Black C

PANTONE 1635 C
PANTONE Process Black C

PANTONE 394 C
PANTONE Process Black C

2. AD, D: Masayuki Uchida DF: Voltage Co. , Ltd. CL: Mitsui O. S. K. Lines, Ltd.   Japan 1995

PANTONE 716 U
PANTONE 304 U

PANTONE 380 U
PANTONE 716 U

PANTONE 304 U
PANTONE 402 U

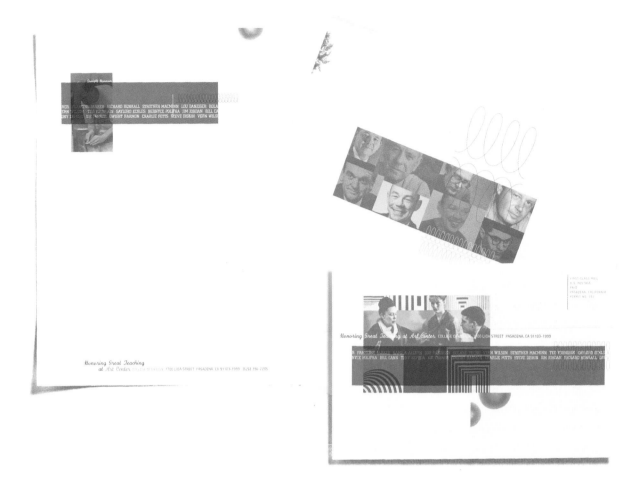

PANTONE 384 U
PANTONE 166 U

1. CD: Stuart I. Frolick AD: Denise Gonzales Crisp DF: Art Center College of Design - Design Office CL: Art Center College of Design   USA 1998

PANTONE 313 U
PANTONE 395 U

2. AD, D, P: Heather Heflin P: J. Malecki / K. Smith DF: Cornish College of the Arts, Publications Dept. CL: Cornish College of the Arts   USA 1997

1. CD: Pattie Belle Hastings D: Bjorn Akselsen DF: Icehouse Design CL: Captain Planet Foundation   USA 1996

PANTONE Reflex Blue U
PANTONE 577 U

2. CD, AD, D: R. Verkaart DF: Stoere Binken Design CL: 3 Some   Netherlands 1997

PANTONE Red 032 C
PANTONE 281 U

3. CD, AD, D: Thomas Neeser / Thomas Müller DF: Neeser + Müller CL: Cycle Sports   Switzerland 1998

PANTONE 249 U
PANTONE 284 U

PANTONE 480 U
PANTONE 583 U CD, AD, D, P, I, CW, DF: Michela Pizzinat   Italy 1997

PANTONE 103 U
PANTONE 289 U D: Ron Faas / Tirso Francés / Tanja Kumpermondt DF: Dietwee CL: Jazzradio   Netherlands 1997

1. CD, AD, D: Kristina Teubner / Katrin Wiens DF: Tour - Salon CL: Held & Seeler Gestaltung   Germany 1998

PANTONE 352 U
PANTONE 498 U

2. CD, AD, D: Anja Osterwalder DF, CL: I - D Büro GmbH   Germany 1997

PANTONE 1495 C
PANTONE Process Black C

PANTONE 3125 C
PANTONE Process Black C

3. CD, AD, D: Anja Osterwalder DF, CL : I - D Büro GmbH   Germany 1998

PANTONE 460 C
PANTONE 534 C

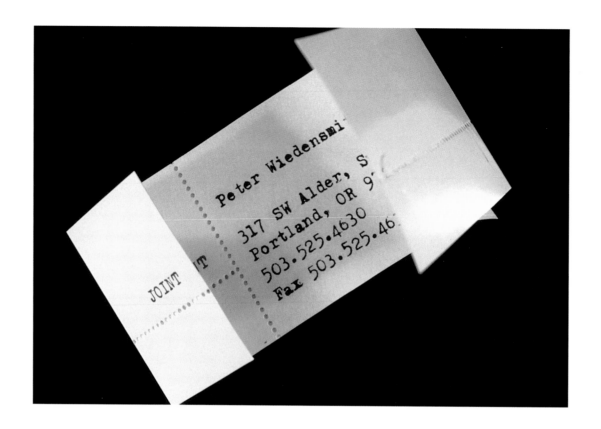

PANTONE Process Black U
PANTONE 485 U

AD, D: Niko Courtelis Printing: Pete McCracken DF: Plazm CL: Joint USA 1997

1.CD, AD, D: Carlos Segura D: Brent Riley / Jim Marcus / Susana Detembleque
DF: Segura Inc. CL: [T - 26] Digital Typefoundry   USA 1997 - 98

PANTONE 1817 U	PANTONE 259 U	PANTONE 877 U	PANTONE 638 U	PANTONE 1935 U	

2. CD, AD, D: Carlos Segura D: Brent Riley / Colin Metcalf
DF: Segura Inc. CL: [T - 26] Digital Typefoundries   USA 1997

PANTONE Process Black U	PANTONE Process Black U	PANTONE Process Black U / PANTONE 141 U	PANTONE Warm Red U	

 PANTONE 185 U
PANTONE Process Black U

1. DF: Clemens Metzler, Dipl. Graphic - Designer CL: Preussag Anthrazit   Germany 1995

 PANTONE 715 U   PANTONE 668 U
PANTONE 646 U   PANTONE 128 U

2. CD, AD, D, I: John Sayles DF: Sayles Graphic Design CL: Gianna Rose   USA 1998

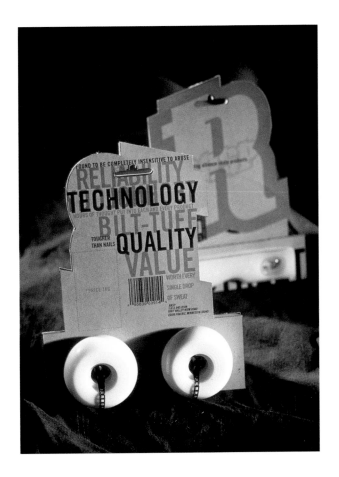

1. CD, D, CW: Steven Sikora D: Mitch Morse DF: Design Guys CL: Midcoast Products   USA 1997

PANTONE Process Black U
PANTONE 165 U

2. CD: Steven Sikora D: Amy Kirkpatrick DF: Design Guys CL: Rollerblade   USA 1998

PANTONE 287 U
PANTONE Warm Red U

PANTONE 144 C
PANTONE Reflex Blue C
PANTONE 877 U

AD: Nick Crosbie D: Inflate Studio / Simon Clark DF: Inflate Studio / Beef CL: Inflate   UK 1998

1. CD, AD, D, DF: Ryan McGinness CW, CL: Schwa   USA 1994

PANTONE 877 C

PANTONE 2738 C

2.3. CD, AD, D: Gary Haslam DF: Rage Corporation CL: Moving Shadow   UK 1998

PANTONE Process Cyan U

PANTONE Process Magenta U

PANTONE 288 U

PANTONE Process Black U

PANTONE Process Blue C   PANTONE 361 C   1. 2. CD, AD: Takahisa Kamiya DF: Super Planning Co. , Ltd. CL: Champ Co. , Ltd.   Japan 1997 (1), 1998 (2)

PANTONE 1235 C   PANTONE 356 C   PANTONE 186 C   3. CD: Satoru Miyata AD: Hatsuyo Egawa D: Noboru Naito I: Tetsuro Okabe CL: Mos Food Service   Japan 1997

| PANTONE 186 C | PANTONE 356 C | PANTONE 1235 C | PANTONE 188 C |

CD: Satoru Miyata AD: Hatsuyo Egawa D: Noboru Naito I: Tetsuro Okabe CL: Mos Food Service   Japan 1997

CD: Frank Luebke AD: Alexandre Janvier CW: Gerrit Schwerzel CL: Rempen & Partner Munich   Germany 1998

PANTONE 186 C
White

PANTONE 186 C
PANTONE Process Black C

INDEX OF SUBMITTORS

PANTONE® 182 C

PANTONE®
872C

PANTONE®
810U

1&2 色グラフィックス Vol.2

Jacket design
Cyan Berlin

Designers
Yutaka Ichimura / Yuka Tamaki

Editors
Kaoru Yamashita / Jun Yonami

Photographer
Kuniharu Fujimoto

Translators
Douglas Allsopp / Setsuko Noguchi

Typesetter
Kenichi Hayakawa

Publisher
Shingo Miyoshi

1
+
2

color graphics vol.2

1999年1月29日初版第1刷発行

発行所　ピエ・ブックス
〒170-0003 東京都豊島区駒込4-14-6 #301
編集 TEL:03-3949-5010 FAX:03-3949-5650
営業 TEL:03-3940-8302 FAX:03-3576-7361
e-mail:piebooks@bekkoame.ne.jp

ISBN4-89444-093-8 C3070
Printed in Japan

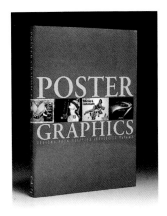

POSTER GRAPHICS Vol. 2
好評！業種別世界のポスター集大成、第2弾
Pages: 256（192 in color）￥16,505＋Tax
700 posters from the top creators in Japan and abroad are showcased in this book - classified by business. This invaluable reference makes it easy to compare design trends among various industries and corporations.

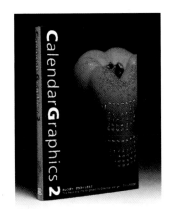

CALENDAR GRAPHICS Vol. 2
好評カレンダー・デザイン集の決定版、第2弾
Pages: 224（192 in Color）￥15,534＋Tax
The second volume of our popular 'Calendar Graphics' series features designs from about 250 1994 and 1995 calendars from around the world. A special collection that includes mass market as well as exclusive corporate PR calendars.

BROCHURE & PAMPHLET COLLECTION Vol. 4
好評！業種別カタログ・コレクション、第4弾
Pages: 224（Full Color）￥15,534＋Tax
The fourth volume in our popular 'Brochure & Pamphlet' series. Twelve types of businesses are represented through artwork that really sells. This book conveys a sense of what's happening right now in the catalog design scene. A must for all creators.

BROCHURE DESIGN FORUM Vol. 3
世界の最新カタログ・コレクション、第3弾
Pages: 224（Full Color）￥15,534＋Tax
A special edition of our 'Brochure & Pamphlet Collection' featuring 250 choice pieces that represent 70 types of businesses and are classified by business for handy reference. A compendium of the design scene at a glance.

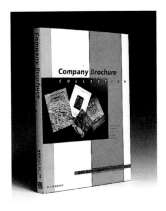

COMPANY BROCHURE COLLECTION
業種別（会社・学校・施設）案内グラフィックス
Pages: 224（192 in Color）￥15,534＋Tax
A special selection of brochures and catalogs ranging from admission manuals for colleges and universities, to amusement facility and hotel guidebooks, to corporate and organization profiles. The entries are classified by industry for easy reference.

COMPANY BROCHURE COLLECTION Vol. 2
業種別会社案内グラフィックス、第2弾！
Pages: 224（Full Color）￥15,534＋Tax
Showing imaginative layouts that present information clearly in a limited space, and design that effectively enhances corporate identity, this volume will prove to be an essential source book for graphic design work of the future.

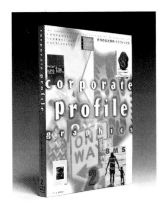

CORPORATE PROFILE GRAPHICS Vol. 2
世界の会社案内グラフィックス、第2弾
Pages: 224（Full Color）￥15,534＋Tax
An extensive collection of company brochures, annual reports, school facility guides and organization pamphlets. Brochures are fully detailed from cover to inner pages, illustrating clearly the importance of cohesiveness and flow. An essential catalog design reference volume.

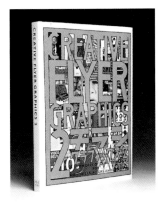

CREATIVE FLYER GRAPHICS Vol. 2
世界のフライヤーデザイン傑作集
Pages: 224（Full Color）￥15,534＋Tax
A pack of some 600 flyers and leaflets incorporating information from a variety of events including exhibitions, movies, plays, concerts, live entertainment and club events, as well as foods, cosmetics, electrical merchandise and travel packages.

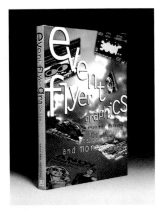

EVENT FLYER GRAPHICS
世界のイベントフライヤー・コレクション
Pages: 224（Full Color）￥15,534＋Tax
Here's a special selection focusing on flyers promoting events. This upbeat selection covers a wide range of music events, as well as movies, exhibitions and the performing arts.

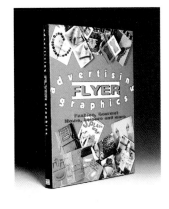

ADVERTISING FLYER GRAPHICS
衣・食・住・遊の商品チラシ特集
Pages: 224（Full Color）￥15,534＋Tax
The eye-catching flyers selected for this new collection represent a broad spectrum of businesses, and are presented in a loose classification covering four essential modern lifestyle themes: fashion, dining, home and leisure.

TRAVEL & LEISURE GRAPHICS
ホテル＆旅行案内グラフィックス
Pages: 224（Full Color）￥15,534＋Tax
A giant collection of some 400 pamphlets, posters and direct mailings exclusively created for hotels, inns, resort tours and amusement facilities

SPECIAL EVENT GRAPHICS
世界のイベント・グラフィックス
Pages: 224（192 in Color）￥15,534＋Tax
A showcase for event graphics, introducing leaflets for exhibitions, fashion shows, all sorts of sales promotional campaigns, posters, premiums and actual installation scenes from events around the world. An invaluable and inspirational resource book, unique in the world of graphic publishing.

1, 2 & 3 COLOR GRAPHICS Vol. 2
1・2・3色グラフィックス、第2弾
Pages: 224 (Full Color) ¥15,534＋Tax
Even more ambitious in scale than the first volume, this second collection of graphics displays the unique talents of graphic designers who work with limited colors. An essential reference guide to effective, low-cost designing.

1 & 2 COLOR GRAPHICS
1色＆2色デザインの大特集
Pages: 224 (Full Color) ¥15,534＋Tax
Powerful design achieved by restricting colors, unusual combinations of colors that grab the attention, enhanced stylishness of script... all artwork featured in this worldwide collection makes a dramatic visual impact. A useful book, too, for exploring the possibilities of low-cost design.

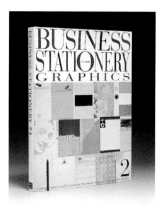

BUSINESS STATIONERY GRAPHICS Vol. 2
世界のレターヘッド・コレクション、第2弾
Pages: 224 (172 in Color) ¥15,534＋Tax
The second volume in our popular "Business Stationery Graphics" series. This publication focuses on letterheads, envelopes and business cards, all classified by business. This collection will serve artists and business people well.

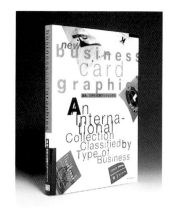

NEW BUSINESS CARD GRAPHICS
最新版！ビジネスカード・グラフィックス
Pages: 224 (Full Color) ¥15,534＋Tax
A selection of 900 samples representing the works of top designers worldwide. Covering the broadest spectrum of business cards, it ranges from the trendiest to the most classy and includes highly original examples along the way.

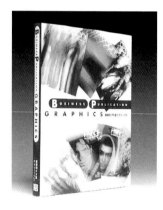

BUSINESS PUBLICATION GRAPHICS
業種別企業PR誌・フリーペーパーの集大成！
Pages: 224 (Full Color) ¥15,534＋Tax
This comprehensive graphic book introduces business publications created for a variety of business needs, including promotions from boutiques and department stores, exclusive clubs, local communities, and company newsletters.

BUSINESS PUBLICATION GRAPHICS Vol. 2
大好評！業種別PR誌の集大成、第2弾
Pages: 224 (Full Color) ¥15,534＋Tax
One volume offering more than 150 samples of regularly published PR and other informative magazines, covering different business sectors from fashion labels to non-profit organizations. This overviews the current trends in PR magazine design aimed at attracting the attention of a specific readership in commercial activities.

POSTCARD GRAPHICS Vol. 4
世界の業種別ポストカード・コレクション
Pages: 224 (192 in Color) ¥15,534＋Tax
Our popular "Postcard Graphics" series has been revamped for "Postcard Graphics Vol. 4." This first volume of the new version showcases approximately 1,000 pieces ranging from direct mailers to private greeting cards, selected from the best around the world.

SEASONAL CAMPAIGN GRAPHICS
デパート・ショップのキャンペーン広告特集
Pages: 224 (Full Color) ¥15,534＋Tax
A spirited collection of quality graphics for sales campaigns planned around the four seasons, Christmas, St. Valentine's Day and the Japanese gift-giving seasons, as well as for store openings, anniversaries, and similar events.

SHOPPING BAG GRAPHICS
世界の最新ショッピングバッグ・デザイン集
Pages: 224 (Full Color) ¥15,534＋Tax
Over 500 samples of the latest and best of the world's shopping bag designs from a wide range of retail businesses! This volume features a selection of shopping bags originating in Tokyo, NY, LA, London, Paris, Milan, and other major cities worldwide, presented here in a useful business classification.

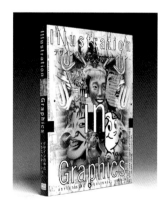

ILLUSTRATION IN GRAPHICS
イラストレーションを使った広告特集
Pages: 224 (Full Color) ¥15,534＋Tax
Delivering the message faster than photos and more accurately than words, illustration never fails to stir the imagination. This superb selection presents some 600 first-class illustrations for advertising from across the business spectrum and for editorial designs.

PRESENTATION GRAPHICS
制作の現場 プレゼンテーション・グラフィックス
Pages: 224 (Full Color) ¥15,500＋Tax
31 designers from 8 countries explain the production side of the creative process. Here are idea sketches, comps, presentations, and final works, all with explanatory notes by the designer. This is a unique volume that peeks behind the scenes of the creator's world.

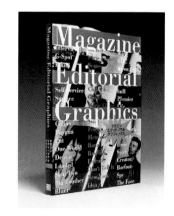

MAGAZINE EDITORIAL GRAPHICS
世界のエディトリアル＆カバーデザイン特集
Pages: 224 (Full Color) ¥15,500＋Tax
A special collection of editorial and cover designs. Stylish and sophisticated, 79 topical books from 9 countries were selected. Including top creators graphic works, innovative fashion photography, and the latest typography, this is a true creator's bible for the New Age.

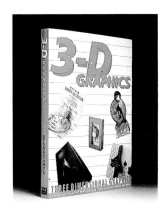

3-D GRAPHICS
3Dグラフィックスの大百科
Pages: 224 (192 in Color) ￥15,534＋Tax
350 works that demonstrate some of the
finest examples of 3-D graphic methods,
including DMs, catalogs, posters, POPs and
more. The volume is a virtual encyclopedia of
3-D graphics.

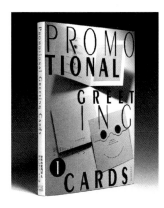

PROMOTIONAL GREETING CARDS
ADVERTISING GREETING CARDS Vol. 4
（English Title）
世界の案内状＆ダイレクトメール集大成
Pages: 224 (Full Color) ￥15,534＋Tax
A total of 500 examples of cards from
designers around the world. A whole
spectrum of stylish and inspirational cards,
classified by function for easy reference.

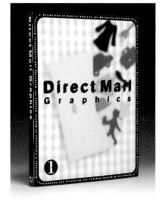

DIRECT MAIL GRAPHICS Vol. 1
衣・食・住のセールスDM特集
Pages: 224 (Full Color) ￥15,534＋Tax
The long-awaited design collection featuring
direct mailers that have outstanding sales
impact and quality design. 350 of the best
pieces, classified into 100 business
categories. A veritable textbook of current
direct marketing design.

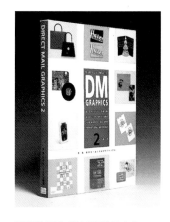

DIRECT MAIL GRAPHICS Vol. 2
好評！衣・食・住のセールスDM特集！第2弾
Pages: 224 (Full Color) ￥15,534＋Tax
The second volume in our extremely popular
"Direct Mail Graphics" series features a
whole range of direct mailers for various
purposes; from commercial announcements
to seasonal greetings. Classfied by industry.

SUCCESSFUL DIRECT MAIL DESIGN
セールス効果の高いDMデザイン集！
Pages: 224 (Full Color) ￥15,500＋Tax
This collection features product flyers,
service guides, shop opening and sale
announcements, school and industrial
promotions, and a variety of event invitations.
A valuable book that captures the essence of
today's direct marketing design.

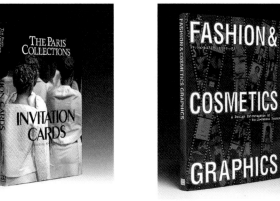

The Paris Collections / INVITATION CARDS
パリ・コレクションの招待状グラフィックス
Pages: 176 (Full Color) ￥13,396＋Tax
This book features 400 announcements for
and invitations to the Paris Collections,
produced by the world's top names in
fashion over the past 10 years. A treasure
trove of ideas and pure fun to browse
through.

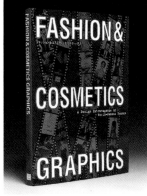

FASHION & COSMETICS GRAPHICS
ファッション＆コスメティック・グラフィックス
Pages: 208 (Full Color) ￥15,534＋Tax
A collection of promotional graphics from
around the world produced for apparel,
accessory and cosmetic brands at the
avantgarde of the fashion industry. 40
brands featured in this book point the way
toward future trends in advertising.

THE TOKYO TYPEDIRECTORS CLUB ANNUAL 1995-96
TDC 年鑑95-96
Pages: 250 (Full Color) ￥16,505＋Tax
A follow-up publication to Japan's only
international graphic deisgn competition.
Featuring 650 typographic artworks selected
by THE TOKYO TYPEDIRECTORS CLUB, this
book provides a window to the latest
typographic design concepts worldwide.

The Production Index ARTIFILE Vol. 5
最新版プロダクション・クリエイター年鑑
Pages: 224 (Full Color) ￥12,136＋Tax
ARTIFILE 5 features artwork from a total of
100 top Japanese production companies and
designers, along with company data and
messages from the creators. An invaluable
information source for anyone who needs to
keep up with the latest developments in the
graphic scene.

CARTOON CHARACTER COLLECTION
5500種のキャラクターデザイン大百科
Pages: 480 (B&W) ￥3,600＋Tax
A collection of illustrations from successful
character artists. People, animals, plants, food,
vehicles, landscapes, sports, seasons.. Nearly
5,500 works are presented, conveniently
categorized. A collection full of ideas sure to
come in handy when designing greeting cards
and illustrations.

CATALOGUE AND PAMPHLET COLLECTION
/ Soft Jacket
業種別商品カタログ特集／ソフトカバー
Pages: 224 (Full Color) ￥3,689＋Tax
A collection of the world's most outstanding
brochures, catalogs and leaflets classified by
industry such as fashion, restaurants, music,
interiors and sporting goods. Presenting each
piece in detail from cover to inside pages.
This title is an indispensable sourcebook for
all graphic designers and CI professionals.

SPORTS GRAPHICS / Soft Jacket
世界のスポーツグッズ・コレクション
／ソフトカバー
Pages: 224 (192 in Color) ￥3,689＋Tax
A Collection of 1,000 bold sporting goods
graphic works from all over the world. A wide
variety of goods, including uniforms, bags,
shoes and other gear. Covers all sorts of
sports: basketball, skiing, surfing, and many
many more.

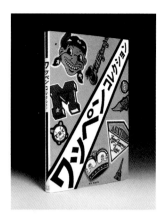

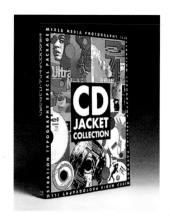

LABELS AND TAGS COLLECTION Vol. 1 / Soft Jacket
ラベル＆タグ・コレクション／ソフトカバー
Pages: 224 (192 in Color) ￥3,689＋Tax
Nowhere is brand recognition more important than in Japan. Here is a collection of 1,600 labels and tags from Japan's 450 top fashion names with page after page of women's and men's clothing and sportswear designs.

FASHION INSIGNIA COLLECTION / Soft Jacket
ワッペン・コレクション／ソフトカバー
Pages: 224 (Full Color) ￥3,689＋Tax
Over 300 designs were scrutinized for this collection of 1000 outstanding emblems and embroidered motifs. Visually exciting, they make innovative use of materials and compliment the fashions with which they are worn.

CD JACKET COLLECTION / Soft Jacket
世界のCDジャケット・コレクション ／ソフトカバー
Pages: 224 (192 in Color) ￥3,689＋Tax
Featuring 700 of the world's most imaginative CD and LP covers from all musical genres, this is a must-have book for all design and music professionals.

POSTCARD COLLECTION Vol. 2 / Soft Jacket
好評 ポストカード・コレクション、第2弾 ／ソフトカバー
Pages: 230 (Full Color) ￥3,689＋Tax
Welcome to the colorful world of postcards, with 1200 postcards created by artists from all over the world classified according to the business of the client.

POSTCARD COLLECTION / Soft Jacket
世界のポストカード・コレクション ／ソフトカバー
Pages: 240 (Full Color) ￥3,689＋Tax
Postcards from top Japanese designers, fashion brands, and famous shops. This book shows how designers, using beautiful photos and fun illustrations, pack a lot of creativity into a postcard's limited space.

DIAGRAM COLLECTION
世界のダイアグラム・デザイン集大成
Pages: 224 (192 in Color) ￥3,700＋Tax
Graphs, charts, maps, architectural diagrams and plans, product and scientific illustrations. Almost 400 diagrams selected from designs sent to us by some of the world's most talented creators. This invaluable volume shows the many possibilities of diagram design.

WORLD BUSINESS CARD COLLECTION
世界の名刺コレクション Vol. 2
Pages: 224 (192 in Color) ￥3,700＋Tax
From personal and business cards, bursting with individuality, to colorfully creative shop cards, we introduce nearly 1,000 of the best. Limited in size, these designs mix fun and cleverness, and will impress and delight you with their originality.

カタログ・新刊のご案内について

総合カタログ、新刊案内をご希望の方は、はさみ込みのアンケートはがきを ご返送いただくか、90円切手同封の上、ピエ・ブックス宛お申し込み下さい。

CATALOGUES ET INFORMATIONS SUR LES NOUVELLES PUBLICATIONS

Si vous désirez recevoir un exemplaire gratuit de notre catalogue général ou des détails sur nos nouvelles publications, veuillez compléter la carte réponse incluse et nous la retourner par courrierou par fax.

CATALOGS and INFORMATION ON NEW PUBLICATIONS

If you would like to receive a free copy of our general catalog or details of our new publications, please fill out the enclosed postcard and return it to us by mail or fax.

CATALOGE und INFORMATIONEN ÜBER NEUE TITLE

Wenn Sie unseren Gesamtkatalog oder Detailinformationen über unsere neuen Titel wünschen, fullen Sie bitte die beigefügte Postkarte aus und schicken Sie sie uns per Post oder Fax.

ピエ・ブックス
〒170 東京都豊島区駒込 4-14-6-301
TEL: 03-3940-8302 FAX: 03-3576-7361

P·I·E BOOKS
#301, 4-14-6, Komagome, Toshima-ku, Tokyo 170 JAPAN
TEL: 03-3940-8302 FAX: 03-3576-7361